UNDERSTANDING THE

# New Testament
# Book by Book

UNDERSTANDING THE

# New Testament
# Book by Book

PETER PAUL JOHN

GOOD NEWS PUBLISHERS
Westchester, Illinois

UNDERSTANDING THE NEW TESTAMENT BOOK BY BOOK
Copyright © 1977 by Peter Paul John
Westchester, Illinois 60153
All rights reserved.
Printed in the United States of America.
Library of Congress Catalog Card Number 77-81559
ISBN 0-89107-151-2

This volume is dedicated to my beloved wife, Marianne, who spent countless hours alone, without complaining or murmuring, as the work was compiled. And this work is offered to the glory of God and the Lord Jesus Christ the "Living Word," who cannot be known apart from his "Written Word," the Bible.

# CONTENTS

# PREFACE

On July 13, 1972, in the tenth year after my conversion, I was privileged to have a heart attack. Five weeks in three hospitals were followed by a three months' convalescence. During this period I asked the Lord, "What do you have in mind for me? What do you want me to learn from this experience?" There developed an intense fellowship with Him in my daily Bible study and, little by little, I began to make an outline of each book of the Bible. Over the next three years this outline materialized.

I am indebted to many authors and expositors whose publications have helped me to a better understanding of the Bible. I gratefully acknowledge the following, from whose writings selected portions appear: *Explore the Book,* J. Sidlow Baxter, Zondervan Publishing House, Grand Rapids, Michigan; *Through the Bible,* J. Vernon McGee, Box 100, Arroyo Annex, Pasadena, California 91109; *The Bible Book by Book,* G. Coleman Luck, Moody Press, 820 North LaSalle, Chicago, Illinois 60610; *Old and New Testament Studies,* Charles J. Woodbridge, The News Publishers, Curwensville, Pennsylvania.

I also am indebted to three men used by the Lord to greatly influence my life.

First, John E. Gardis, my attorney, who confronted me with the claims of Jesus Christ, leading to my salvation.

Second, H. Clay Conner, an insurance executive and Sunday school instructor in my Christian childhood, who grounded me in the Bible and instilled a desire to teach others.

Third, Jack C. Brown, another attorney, who through the years has exemplified Proverbs 27:17, "Iron sharpeneth iron; so a man sharpeneth the countenance of his friend." He has had a tremendous sharpening effect upon me, encouraging and exhorting me to greater service to my Lord. In addition, he corrected, edited and proofed this work.

Peter Paul John
Indianapolis, Indiana

# INTRODUCTION

There are various methods of Bible study:

- *Theological method*—trace key doctrinal points through the Bible.
- *Topical method*—trace a subject or a theme, such as "righteousness," "works," "faith."
- *Biographical method*—study individuals in the Bible.
- *Comparative method*—compare one verse or verses with another verse or verses.
- *Survey method*—read through the Bible in its entirety watching how each book relates to the others, getting an over view of the Bible.
- *Analytical method*—break each book into its component parts.

In this compilation I have chosen the *analytical method* to help you in *Understanding the New Testament, Book by Book.* In studying the Bible, if you are a Christian, ask the Lord, through His Holy Spirit, to open the eyes of your understanding ... (Ephesians 1:18) and to "give unto you the spirit of wisdom and revelation in the knowledge of him" (Ephesians 1:17).

Do not read the Bible with preconceived notions of

what you think it ought to say or what you want it to say. Do not take passages out of context. Do not separate one verse from the rest of the verses in a given passage of scripture. Do not base a doctrinal point upon just one verse of scripture, but take the consensus of several passages of scripture touching on that doctrine.

In order to understand the Bible better it is important to consider the history, customs and cultures of the time of each book. In each verse know who is speaking as well as to whom he is speaking, that is, Jew, Gentile or believer, whether Jew or Gentile. God deals with the Jews one way, the Gentiles another, and the Church (body of believers) another. These suggestions will assist in *Understanding the New Testament, Book by Book.*

It is my prayer that the reader will be challenged to "search the scriptures" in order to come to know Jesus Christ as personal Lord and Savior. It also is my hope that if you are already a believer, you will "study to show yourself approved" (II Timothy 2:15), in order that you may be "ready always to give an answer to every man that asketh you a reason of the hope that is in you with meekness and of fear" (I Peter 3:15).

Peter Paul John
Indianapolis, Indiana

# MATTHEW

28 Chapters
(1068 Verses)

Key Verses:
Matthew 23:37-39

## WRITTEN BY

Matthew, probably in Judea.

## WRITTEN TO

The Jews (there are 65 references to the Old Testament).

## DATE WRITTEN

Before the destruction of Jerusalem in 70 A.D. (Matt. 24:2). Possibly written in 52-56 A.D.

## PURPOSES OF BOOK

To show that the Lord of the Christians is the Messiah of the Jews and that Jesus of Nazareth is the prophesied Messiah and King of Israel of the Old Testament.

## THEME

Jesus Christ is presented as the King of the Jews, the Messiah, the Lion of Judah.

## BRIEF DESCRIPTION

After tracing Christ's genealogy back to Abraham, Matthew then develops the birth of Jesus and His infancy, His baptism by John the Baptist, His wilderness temptation, the Sermon on the Mount, the Olivet Discourse, His 10 parables and two miracles, His entry into Jerusalem, His rejection by the Jews, His Crucifixion by the Jews and His Resurrection.

## KEY VERSES: MATTHEW 23:37-39

O Jerusalem, Jerusalem, thou that killest the prophets, and stonest them which are sent unto thee, how often would I have gathered thy children together, even as a hen gathereth her chickens under her wings, and ye would not! Behold, your house is left unto you desolate. For I say unto you, Ye shall not see me henceforth, till ye shall say, Blessed is he that cometh in the name of the Lord.

## KEY WORDS

Fulfilled (Fulfill)—17 times
Kindom of Heaven—32 times

## KEY WORD FOR EACH CHAPTER

1. Genealogy
2. Wise Men, Infancy
3. Jesus' Baptism
4. Temptations
5. Sermon
6. Sermon (Lord's Prayer)
7. Sermon (Judge)
8. Jesus' authority
9. Miracles
10. The 12 Apostles
11. John the Baptist
12. Holy Ghost

13. Parables
14. Beheaded
15. Woman of Canaan
16. Peter
17. Transfigured
18. Unmerciful debtor
19. Rich young man
20. Vineyard
21. Entry
22. Wedding feast
23. Scribes and Pharisees
24. Olivet
25. 10 virgins, Talents
26. Last Supper, Betrayal
27. Crucified
28. Risen

## OUTLINE BY THEME

Ch. 1:1-4:16    Preparation of the King
Ch. 4:17-16:20  Proclamation by the King
Ch. 16:21-28:20 Passion (suffering) of the King

## ALTERNATE OUTLINE: BY GEOGRAPHY

Ch. 1:1-4:11    Preparation in Judea
Ch. 4:12-18:35  Ministry in Galilee
Ch. 19:1-20:34  Journey into Judea (beyond Jordan)
Ch. 21:1-28:20  Final week in Jerusalem

## ALTERNATE OUTLINE: BY CONTENT

Ch. 1:1-17     His Ancestry
Ch. 1:18-2:23  His Advent
Ch. 3:1-12     His Ambassador
Ch. 3:13-4:11  His Advance
Ch. 4:12-18    Detour in Galilee
Ch. 5-7        What Jesus taught (said)—Sermon (10 components)

| | |
|---|---|
| Ch. 8-10 | What Jesus wrought (did)— Miracles (10 miracles) |
| Ch. 11-18 | What people thought (results)— Reactions (10 reactions) |
| Ch. 19-25 | Presentation |
| Ch. 19-20 | Journey to city |
| Ch. 21:1-17 | Entry into city |
| Ch. 21:18-23 | Clashes in city |
| Ch. 24-25 | Olivet Discourse |
| Ch. 26, 27 | Crucifixion (Jesus in 4 settings) |
| Ch. 26:1-56 | Among His disciples |
| Ch. 26:57-75 | Before Sanhedrin |
| Ch. 27:1-26 | Before the Roman governor |
| Ch. 27:27-66 | Crucified, Dead and Buried |
| Ch. 28 | Resurrection |
| Ch. 28:1-7 | Intervention of angel |
| Ch. 28:8-10 | Reappearance of risen Lord |
| Ch. 28:11-15 | Lying invention of Jews |
| Ch. 28:16-20 | New Commissioning of 11 Apostles |

## CHAPTER BY CHAPTER

Ch. 1 Genealogy of Jesus; circumstances of His birth

Ch. 2 Jesus' infancy; the wise men; the flight into Egypt

Ch. 3 John's baptism of Jesus

Ch. 4 The temptation in the wilderness; Jesus selects His disciples

Ch. 5 Sermon on the Mount

Ch. 6 Sermon on the Mount

Ch. 7 Sermon on the Mount

# MARK

16 Chapters                        Key Verse:
(678 Verses)                   Mark 10:45

### WRITTEN BY

John Mark, cousin of Barnabas (Col. 4:10), son of Mary, an inhabitant of Jerusalem (Acts 12:12). Mark was not one of the 12 Apostles (Matt. 10:2-4).

### WRITTEN TO

Romans (Gentiles) probably from Rome.

### DATE WRITTEN

Approximately 50-55 A.D.

### PURPOSE OF BOOK

To present the Lord Jesus Christ as the unique, perfect and faithful Son of God as He ministered in His daily life with all the fullness of the Servant who stooped to serve and to conquer (Zech. 3:8).

19

## THEME

Jesus Christ, the Son of God, is presented as God's Suffering Servant who performs 22 miracles.

## BRIEF DESCRIPTION

There are 22 miracles recorded as Jesus Christ is portrayed as the Son of God going about in His daily life ministering unto the needs of the people. There are only six parables narrated. Jesus is constantly on the go performing miracles. He was so busy that Mark even that says the Apostles "had no leisure so much as to eat." The word "straightway" (immediately) is used over 40 times. Jesus is described as having to retire from His enemies or to refresh His soul with prayer no less than 11 times. The betrayal of Judas, the denial of Peter, the Crucifixion, Death, burial and Resurrection are told.

## KEY VERSE: MARK 10:45

For even the Son of man came not to be ministered unto, but to minister, and to give his life a ransom for many.

## KEY WORD

Immediately (straightway)—40 times

## KEY WORD FOR EACH CHAPTER

Because of the unusual amount of activity of the Lord Jesus described by Mark, it is difficult to select one or even two key words for each chapter. This is also the reason for the detailed breakdown of each chapter.

## OUTLINE

| | |
|---|---|
| Ch. 1:1-13 | The Preparation of the Servant |
| Ch. 1:14-8:26 | The Work of the Servant |
| Ch. 8:27-15:47 | The Suffering of the Servant |
| Ch. 16:1-20 | The Victory of the Servant |

## CHAPTER BY CHAPTER

| | |
|---|---|
| Ch. 1:1-8 | John the Baptist |
| Ch. 1:9-11 | Jesus is baptized |
| Ch. 1:12-13 | Temptation in the wilderness |
| Ch. 1:14-20 | Jesus calls His disciples |
| Ch. 1:21-45 | Miracles performed |
| Ch. 2:1-13 | Miracles performed |
| Ch. 2:14-17 | Matthew called, Jesus eats with sinners |
| Ch. 2:18-28 | Jesus and the Pharisees |
| Ch. 3:1-13 | Miracles performed |
| Ch. 3:14-19 | The 12 Apostles chosen |
| Ch. 3:20-35 | Jesus warns the scribes |
| Ch. 4:1-34 | Four parables |
| Ch. 4:35-6:6 | Miracles performed |
| Ch. 6:7-13 | The 12 Apostles sent forth two by two |
| Ch. 6:14-30 | John the Baptist beheaded |
| Ch. 6:31-56 | Miracles performed |
| Ch. 7:1-13 | Jesus and the Pharisees and scribes |
| Ch. 7:14-8:26 | Miracles performed |
| Ch. 8:27-33 | Peter's Confession of faith |
| Ch. 8:34-38 | Jesus talks to the people and His disciples |
| Ch. 9:1-10 | Jesus' Transfiguration |
| Ch. 9:11-32 | Miracle performed |
| Ch. 9:33-50 | Teaching and warning |
| Ch. 10:1-31 | Varied teachings |
| Ch. 10:32-52 | On the way to Jerusalem |
| Ch. 11:1-11 | The triumphal entry |
| Ch. 11:12-33 | Various experiences in and near Jerusalem |
| Ch. 12:1-40 | Parables and questions |
| Ch. 12:40-44 | The widow's mite |

# LUKE

24 Chapters            Key Verse:
(1151 Verses)            Luke 19:10

### WRITTEN BY

Luke, a Gentile (probably Greek) medical doctor. He was not one of the 12 Apostles (Matt. 10:2-4).

### WRITTEN TO

Theophilus (the name, in Greek, means "friend of God") who probably was a Greek (Gentile) nobleman and high government official.

Matthew wrote for Jews; Mark wrote for Romans; and Luke wrote for Greeks (Luke 1:1-4; Acts 1:1). These represent the three great history-shaping peoples of that time: the Romans in law, the Jews in religion and the Greeks in literature and art.

### DATE WRITTEN

Approximately 60 A.D., probably from Caesarea.

### PURPOSE OF BOOK

Luke's purpose is stated in his Prologue (1:1-4) as he traces the course "of all things from the very first" accurately and writes "in order" (in chronological sequence) so that the reader might "know the certainty of those things, wherein thou hast been instructed."

## THEME

Jesus Christ in His humanity is depicted as the Son of Man who came "to seek and to save that which was lost" (Israel) (Luke 19:10).

## BRIEF DESCRIPTION

Luke covers a period of approximately 35 years of the words and deeds of the Lord Jesus, from the announcement by an angel of the Lord to Zacharias concerning John the Baptist's birth to the Lord's Ascension into heaven.

## KEY VERSE: LUKE 19:10

For the Son of man is come to seek and to save that which was lost.

## KEY WORD

Son of Man—26 times. This title speaks of more than His humanity. It speaks of Him being the perfect Man, the only true representative of the entire human race.

## KEY WORDS FOR EACH CHAPTER

1. Zacharias, Elisabeth
2. Decree, Simeon, Anna
3. John, Son
4. Wilderness, Synagogue
5. Launch out
6. Heal, Sermon
7. Capernaum, John
8. Sower, Legion
9. Power, Son, Peter, Moses
10. Seventy, Samaritan

11. Pray, Casting
12. Hypocrisy
13. Woman, Mustard seed
14. Dropsy, Supper
15. Sheep, Coin, Prodigal
16. Rich man, Lazarus
17. Lepers, Kingdom
18. Judge, Publican, Ruler
19. Zacchaeus, Nobleman, 10 Servants
20. Husbandmen, Penny, Sadducees
21. Mites, Nation, Fig
22. Passover, Denied
23. Pilate, Cross
24. Emmaus

## OUTLINE

| | |
|---|---|
| Ch. 1:1-4 | Introduction (Prologue) |
| Ch. 1:5-2:52 | Background (Announcement and Advent) of the Son of Man |
| Ch. 3:1-4:13 | Beginning of the mission of the Son of Man |
| Ch. 4:14-9:50 | His ministry in Galilee |
| Ch. 9:51-19:48 | His journey to Jerusalem |
| Ch. 19:45-23:56 | His last week in Jerusalem |
| Ch. 24 | His Resurrection and Ascension |

## CHAPTER BY CHAPTER

Ch. 1 The births of John the Baptist and the Lord Jesus announced; John the Baptist is born.

Ch. 2 Jesus is born; Jesus, as a child, in the Temple.

Ch. 3 John the Baptist preaches repentance; Jesus is baptized; the Genealogy of Christ back to Adam.

Ch. 4 Jesus is tempted in the wilderness; Jesus is rejected at Nazareth; He teaches and heals in Galilee.

little children; Jesus and the ruler; Jesus heals a blind man.

Ch. 19 Jesus and Zacchaeus; parable of the nobleman and his 10 servants; Jesus enters Jerusalem upon a colt; temple cleansed.

Ch. 20 The parable of the wicked husbandmen; Jesus, the chief priests and scribes and the penny; Jesus and the Sadducees.

Ch. 21 The widow's mites; His last prophetic discourse; parable of the fig tree.

Ch. 22 The Last Supper; Judas betrays Christ; Peter denies Christ; Jesus before the council.

Ch. 23 Christ's trial; Christ's Crucifixion and burial.

Ch. 24 The empty tomb; the road to Emmaus; Christ's appearance before His disciples; His Ascension.

# JOHN

| | |
|---|---|
| 21 Chapters | Key Verse: |
| (879 Verses) | John 20:31 |

## WRITTEN BY

John, the beloved Apostle, son of Zebedee.

## WRITTEN TO

All people everywhere.

## DATE WRITTEN

Approximately 90 A.D.

## PURPOSE OF BOOK

To establish the deity of Christ (1:1-18) through His words and His deeds in order that the reader "might believe that Jesus is the Christ and that believing ye might have life through His name" (20:31).

## THEME

The words and deeds of Jesus Christ demonstrating the power of God; His Death and Resurrection.

## BRIEF DESCRIPTION

Jesus' life is depicted through seven miracles which He performs starting from His early ministry in Cana and also through His words as well as His trial, Death and Resurrection.

## SPECIAL INFORMATION

Words of Jesus (2:22)—I am (Ex. 3:14)

| | |
|---|---|
| Ch. 6:35 | I am the bread of life. |
| Ch. 8:12 | I am the light of the world. |
| Ch. 8:58 | Before Abraham was, I am. |
| Ch. 10:9 | I am the door. |
| Ch. 10:11 | I am the good shepherd. |
| Ch. 11:25 | I am the resurrection, life. |
| Ch. 14:6 | I am the way, truth, life. |
| Ch. 15:1 | I am the vine. |

## KEY VERSE: JOHN 20:31

But these are written that ye might believe that Jesus is the Christ, the Son of God: and that believing ye might have life through his name.

## KEY WORD

Believe—98 times

## KEY WORD FOR EACH CHAPTER

1. Beginning, John
2. Wedding
3. Nicodemus
4. Woman, Nobelman's son — *accept-believe-trust him*
5. Lame man
6. 5,000, Water, Bread
7. Feast
8. Woman, Light
9. Blind man
10. Good Shepherd
11. Lazarus
12. Mary, Psalms, Greeks
13. Feet, Peter
14. Thomas, Philip, Judas

15. Vine
16. Comforter
17. Prayer
18. Betrayed, Denied
19. Crucified
20. Thomas
21. Peter

## OUTLINE

| | |
|---|---|
| Ch. 1:1-18 | Prologue |
| Ch. 1:19-12:59 | Christ's (public) ministry as Life to the World |
| Ch. 13:1-17:26 | Christ's (private) ministry as Light to the Disciples |
| Ch. 18:1-20:31 | Arrest, trial and Resurrection of Christ |
| Ch. 21:1-25 | Epilogue |

## BOOK OF JOHN
## "I AM"
### (Figurative and Symbolical)

| | | | |
|---|---|---|---|
| 1. | Ch. 6:35 | The Bread of Life | Ex. 16:4-35 |
| 2. | Ch. 8:12 | The Light of the World | Ps. 27:1 Is. 60:19 |
| 3. | Ch. 10:9 | The Door | Deut. 28:6 Nu. 27:17 |
| 4. | Ch. 10:11 | The Good Shepherd | Gen. 49:24 Ps. 23 |
| 5. | Ch. 11:25 | The Resurrection | Job 14:14 Job 19:25 Ps. 49:15 Is. 25:8 |
| 6. | Ch. 11:25 | The Life (John 14:6 also) | Ps. 121:8 Ps. 133:3 Is. 25:8 John 17:2, 3 |

31

| 7. Ch. 14:6 | The Way | Deut. 32:39 |
| | | Ps. 68:20 |
| | | Ps. 16:11 |
| | | Is. 35:8 |
| | | Jer. 6:16 |
| 8. Ch. 14:6 | The Truth | Deut. 32:4 |
| | | Ps. 31:5 |
| | | Ps. 33:4 |
| | | Ps. 100:5 |
| 9. Ch. 15:1 | The True Vine | Ps. 80:8 |
| | | Is. 5:7 |
| | | Jer. 2:21 |

**JOHN 8:58** Before Abraham was **I AM**

## DEEDS OF JESUS

Miracles in John demonstate the power of God:

## LORD OF NATURE

| Chapter | In the realm of nature: | Miracle accomplished by: |
|---|---|---|
| 2 | Water into wine | Transformation |
| 6 | Bread and fishes | Multiplication |
| 6 | Great wind and sea | Subjugation |

## MASTER OF DISEASES

| Chapter | In the realm of disease: | Miracle accomplished by: |
|---|---|---|
| 4 | Nobleman's son | Cured from a distance |
| 5 | Lame man | Effected by a command |
| 9 | Blind man | Healed by use of means |
| 11 | Lazarus | Effected by a command |

| Miracles in John | | Changed From | Changed To |
|---|---|---|---|
| 2:1-11 | Water into wine | commonplace | distinction |
| 4:46-54 | Nobleman's son | disease | health |
| 5:1-9 | Lame man | paralysis | vitality |
| 6:1-14 | Feed 5,000 | hunger | satisfaction |
| 6:15-21 | Walk on water | turmoil | calm |
| 9:1-7 | Blind man | darkness | light |
| 11:1-44 | Lazarus | death | life |

## TESTIMONY OF JESUS IN THE WORDS OF OTHERS

| John (author) | Ch. 1:1, 14 | The Word (Jesus) was God |
|---|---|---|
| John the Baptist | Ch. 1:29 | The Lamb of God |
| Andrew | Ch. 1:41 | The Messiah |
| Philip | Ch. 1:45 | Him, of whom Moses and the Prophets wrote |
| Nathaniel | Ch. 1:49 | Son of God, King of Israel |
| Samaritans | Ch. 4:42 | The Christ, the Savior of the world |
| Peter | Ch. 6:68 | The Christ, the Son of the living God |
| Many of the people | Ch. 7:40 | The prophet |
| Officers | Ch. 7:46 | Never man spake like this man |
| Blind man | Ch. 9:35-38 | Worshipped Him as the Son of God |
| Pilate | Ch. 18:38 | I find in Him no fault |
| Thomas | Ch. 20:28 | My Lord and my God |

## 9 STEPS OF PROGRESSIVE REVELATION OF LIFE IN JOHN

| | |
|---|---|
| Ch. 1:4 | Life gives light. |
| Ch. 3:14-15 | Life is through faith and is eternal. |
| Ch. 3:36 | Life is available now. |
| Ch. 4:14 | Life gives inward satisfaction. |
| Ch. 5:24 | Possession of life gives exemption from judgement. |
| Ch. 6:40 | Life gives promise of immortality for the body. |
| Ch. 10:27-29 | Strongest assurance is given that eternal life is eternal preservation. |
| Ch. 17:21 | Eternal life is consumated in a heavenly glorification. |

## CHAPTER BY CHAPTER

Ch. 1 The Word becomes flesh; witness of John the Baptist: Jesus' first disciples.

Ch. 2 Water changed into wine at Cana; temple cleansed at Jerusalem.

Ch. 3 Jesus and Nicodemus; additional testimony from John the Baptist.

Ch. 4 The woman of Samaria; the nobleman's son healed.

Ch. 5 The lame man healed and the critical Jews answered.

Ch. 6 Jesus feeds the 5,000, walks on the water and reveals Himself as the Bread of Life.

Ch. 7 Jesus at the Feast of Tabernacles.

Ch. 8 The adulterous woman forgiven, Jesus' discourse on the Light of the World.

Ch. 9 The healing of the blind man.

Ch. 10 The discourse on the Good Shepherd.

Ch. 11 The raising of Lazarus from the dead.

# ACTS

28 Chapters
(1007 Verses)

Key Verse:
Acts 1:8

### WRITTEN BY

Luke, "the beloved physician" (Col. 4:14). In Acts 16:10-16 the use of the pronouns *we* and *us* indicates Luke was with Paul on his second missionary journey.

### WRITTEN TO

Theophilus (compare Acts 1:1 with Luke 1:3), who was probably a Christian Gentile official in the Roman government. The name Theophilus (in Greek) literally means "friend of God."

### DATE WRITTEN

Approximately 63 A.D.

### TIME PERIOD COVERED

From the post-Resurrection days of the Lord Jesus Christ on earth (Acts 1:3) and His Ascension (Acts 1:10-11) in 30 A.D. to the imprisonment of Paul in Rome in approximately 63 A.D. (approximately 33 years).

## PURPOSES OF BOOK

To show how the risen Lord continued to do from Heaven what He had commenced on earth. In Matthew 16:18, He said, "I will build my church." In Acts He is seen doing so through the Holy Spirit (John 16:7, 14), by using Spirit-controlled men. The message of Peter and Stephen in Acts 2:14-40 and 3:17-21 was a renewed offer of the Messianic Kingdom to Israel. The message of Paul was the "Gospel" (I Cor. 15:1-4), to the Jew and also to the Gentile, and not merely in Jerusalem, but throughout the world. In addition, the purpose of the book of Acts is to show how the Lord continued to make overtures to the Jews with the Kingdom message to repent, and eventually left them to their unbelief in order that the message of salvation might be taken to the Gentiles.

## THEME

The renewed presentation of the Messianic Kingdom by the Apostles to the Jews; their rejection of it; and the history of the development of the early church.

## BRIEF DESCRIPTION

The book of Acts describes how the ascended Lord Jesus continues to work directly with the Holy Spirit who now has come in accordance with His promise (John 16:7), using Spirit-controlled men as His instruments whom He has sent out (John 17:18). Peter is the central figure in the first 12 chapters and Paul is the central figure in the last 16.

## SPECIAL INFORMATION

In the Key Verse, Acts 1:8, the Lord Jesus told His disciples that they would be "witnesses unto me both in Jerusalem, and in all Judea, and in Samaria, and unto the uttermost part of the earth." The witness in

Jerusalem is recorded in chapters 1-7; the witness in Judea and Samaria is recorded in chapters 8-12; the witness in the "uttermost part" is recorded in chapters 13-28.

## KEY VERSE: ACTS 1:8

But ye shall receive power, after that the Holy Ghost is come upon you: and ye shall be witnesses to Me both in Jerusalem, and in all Judea, and in Samaria, and unto the uttermost part of the earth.

## KEY WORDS

Spirit (Holy Ghost)—54 times
Jesus, Lord, Christ—33 times

## KEY WORDS FOR EACH CHAPTER

1. Ascension
2. Pentecost, Peter
3. Lame man, temple
4. Peter and John, Persecution
5. Ananias
6. Seven deacons
7. Stephen
8. Philip and the Eunuch
9. Paul's conversion
10. Cornelius
11. Christians
12. Prayer
13. Missions
14. Iconium
15. Council, Question
16. Philippi, Timothy, Lydia, Jailer
17. Athens, Mars Hill
18. Corinth, Vow, Apollos
19. Ephesus, Demetrius
20. Elders
21. Paul's arrest, Warning

22. Paul's testimony
23. Sanhedrin
24. Felix
25. Festus
26. Paul's testimony before Agrippa
27. Shipwreck
28. Rome

## OUTLINE

| | |
|---|---|
| Ch. 1-8:3 | Message of the Kingdom preached to Israel |
| Ch. 8:4-12:25 | Transition period of the Church |
| Ch. 13-28 | Gentile period of the Church |

## OUTLINE BY PERSONALITIES

| | |
|---|---|
| Ch. 1-12 | The Ministry of Peter and others to the Jews |
| Ch. 13-28 | The Ministry of Paul to the Gentiles |

## TWO PREDOMINANT FIGURES

| Peter | (Paul) | (Peter) | Paul |
|---|---|---|---|
| Central Figure | | | Central Figure |
| Acts 1:1-8:4 | 9:1-21 | 9:32-11:18 | 11:19-28:31 |

Peter's ministry was to the Jews (Gal. 2:7) and he preached the need to "repent and be baptized" (Acts 2:38). Paul's ministry was to the Gentiles (Acts 9:15; Gal. 2:7) and he was called "not of men, neither by man, but by Jesus Christ" (Gal. 1:1). He was not one of the 12 Apostles (Matt. 10:2-4; Acts 1:26, 2:14), but was called "out of due time" (I Cor. 15:8) to preach "the gospel of the grace of God" (Acts 20:24) "which is given me" (Eph. 3:2, 3). He preached "among the Gentiles the unsearchable riches of Christ" (Eph. 3:8).

Acts is not presented in chronological order, and

40

those who have attempted to list the chronology vary
from one to two years in their order. However, Light-
foot's is widely accepted, viz.:

EVENT
1.  Ascension of Christ
2.  Conversion of Saul
3.  Paul's first visit to Jerusalem
4.  Paul at Antioch
5.  Paul's second visit to Jerusalem
6.  Paul's first missionary journey
7.  The Great Council at Jerusalem
8.  Paul's first visit to Corinth
9.  Paul's fourth visit to Jerusalem
10. Paul leaves Ephesus
11. Paul's arrest in Jerusalem
12. Paul reaches Rome
13. Close of the "Acts"
14. Paul is martyred

| CHAPTER | A.D. |
| --- | --- |
| 1:9 | 30 |
| 9:1-19 | 34-36 |
| 9:26 | 37, 38 |
| 11:26 | 44 |
| 11:30 | 45 |
| 13:4 | 48 |
| 15:1-29 | 51 |
| 18:1 | 52 |
| 18:22 | 54 |
| 20:1 | 57 |
| 21:33 | 58 |
| 28:16 | 61 |
| 28:30, 31 | 63 |
| | 67 |

41

*The three missionary journeys of Paul are covered in the book of Acts as follows:*

First Missionary Journey        Acts 13: 4-14:26
Second Missionary Journey      Acts 15:36-18:22
Third Missionary Journey        Acts 18:22-21:15

PART I (1-12)
Jerusalem the center
Peter the chief figure
Out to Samaria
Word rejected by Jews of homeland
Judgment on Herod

PART II (13-28)
Antioch the center
Paul the chief figure
Out to Rome
Word rejected by Jews of Dispersion
Judgment on Jews

## THE THREE PIVOTAL EVENTS
### IN ACTS

1. The Outrage against Stephen (Acts 7:54-60)—In chapters 1-12 everything leads up to or results from the outrage against Stephen.
2. The Outbreak against Paul (Acts 22:22).
3. The Outgoing to the Gentiles (Acts 28:28).

In the early chapters from one to seven, three miracles take place which serve to prepare the way for three messages to the Jews:

Ch. 2:   Miracle of "tongues" followed by Peter's sermon to an all Jewish audience, "Jews, devout men, out of every nation under heaven" (Acts 2:5).

Ch. 3, 4:   Miracle of the lame man walking followed by Peter's message to the Jewish people and leaders which was opposed (Acts 4:2, 3).

Ch. 5: Judgment of Ananias and Sapphira subsequently followed by Peter's message to the high priest and the Jewish Council which was also opposed (Acts 5:33).

*Stephen's address (Acts 7:2-53) is a comprehensive synopsis of Israel's history which was designated to show:*

1. That Christ's rejection was not proof that He was not the Messiah, for Israel's outstanding heroes had frequently been accepted after first having been violently rejected. (Note Moses' rejection in Ex. 2:14; note also Joseph's rejection by his brothers in Gen. 37:23-31).

2. That the Mosaic Covenant (Ex. 19:5, 6) was not a permanent institution. (Jer. 31:31-33; Deut. 18:15-19).

3. That Abraham had enjoyed a close relationship with God long before the Mosaic law. (Gen. 15:6; Gen. 17; Gal. 3:17).

## STEPHEN'S MESSAGE

| | |
|---|---|
| Ch. 7:1-8 | Abrahamic Call and Covenant |
| Ch. 7:9-16 | Joseph and his brothers |
| Ch. 7:17-43 | Moses and the people of Israel (from Egypt to Babylon) |
| Ch. 7:44-50 | The Tabernacle and the Temple |
| Ch. 7:51-53 | Stephen's Indictment against Israel |

Before God left the Jews in their unbelief and took the message of salvation to the Gentiles, He spoke three times to the nation of Israel.

1. He spoke to them through John the Baptist.

2. He spoke to them through Jesus Christ whose death they demanded (Luke 23:18-21).

3. God finally spoke to them through His Holy Spirit (Acts 7:51) filling Stephen whom they murdered (Acts 7:59).

## CHAPTER BY CHAPTER

Ch. 1 The Ascension of Christ and the selection of Matthias as the Apostle to replace Judas.

Ch. 2 The descent of the Holy Spirit to indwell men on the day of Pentecost and Peter's great message.

Ch . 3 The healing of the lame man and Peter's second message.

Ch. 4 Peter and John arrested and threatened by the rulers; the Apostles pray for boldness in witnessing.

Ch. 5 Ananias and Sapphira die for lying to the Holy Spirit; the Apostles are imprisoned, released by an angel of the Lord, brought before the council, threatened, and yet continue to witness boldly.

Ch. 6 The selection of seven men to be used in the daily care of the poor; Stephen, one of the seven, is used mightily.

Ch. 7 Stephen's great message of indictment to Israel; Israel's resistance against the Holy Spirit; Stephen's murder.

Ch. 8 The word is scattered throughout Judea and Samaria because of persecution; Philip and the Ethiopian eunuch.

Ch. 9 The conversion experience of Saul of Tarsus; Peter heals Aeneas and raises Dorcas from the dead.

Ch. 10 Peter and the conversion of the first Gentile, Cornelius.

Ch. 11 Peter recounts to the Apostles how Cornelius

is saved; Barnabas and Saul minister to the church at Antioch.

Ch. 12 James, the brother of John, is martyred; Peter is imprisoned and released by an angel of the Lord; Herod is eaten by worms and dies.

Ch. 13 Barnabas and Paul start on their first missionary journey; sail to Cyprus; encounter a false prophet, Bar-Jesus, at Salamis; return to Antioch where Paul preaches to the Jews who oppose him.

Ch. 14 Paul and Barnabas preach at Iconium; Paul heals the crippled man at Lystra, but is later stoned and left for dead; the Apostles return to Antioch "rehearsing all that God had done with them."

Ch. 15 The Council at Jerusalem repudiates the Judaizers; after contending with Barnabas concerning Mark (who eventually wrote the book of Mark), Paul chooses Silas and they start on their second missionary journey.

Ch. 16 Paul meets Timothy; is directed to go to Macedonia; goes to Philippi where Lydia is converted; casts out the demons from the damsel who was possessed; Paul and Silas cast in prison and the Philippian jailer converted.

Ch. 17 Paul and Silas go to Thessalonica where they are successful; move to Berea; then Paul goes to Athens where he preaches on Mars Hill.

Ch. 18 Paul goes to Corinth and stays 18 months, then goes to Ephesus and returns to Antioch; Paul sets out on his third missionary journey.

Ch. 19 Paul comes to Ephesus, stays there three years (Acts 20:31) and ministers to the people; Demetrius the silversmith causes a riot against Paul.

Ch. 20 Paul continues his travels, comes to Troas where he was "long preaching"; Eutychus falls asleep, falls down and dies, and Paul brings him back from the dead; Paul charges the Ephesian elders.

Ch. 21 Paul goes to Jerusalem against the wishes of the believers in Caesarea; Paul is seized by a Jewish mob who tries to kill him but is saved by the chief captain.

Ch. 22 Paul addresses the mob and gives his testimony.

Ch. 23 Paul speaks to the council; then is sent to Caesarea to Felix the Roman governor.

Ch. 24 Paul defends himself and his doctrine before Felix.

Ch. 25 Paul appears before Festus and appeals to Caesar; Agrippa tells Festus he wants to hear Paul speak.

Ch. 26 Paul speaks before King Agrippa and brings his testimony.

Ch. 27 Paul is shipwrecked on his way to Rome.

Ch. 28 Paul comes to Melita (Malta), is bitten by a venomous snake and is not affected by it, heals Publius' father and many others; then travels to Rome where he speaks to the Jewish leaders; stays in Rome two years "in his own hired home" in considerable liberty.

# ROMANS

16 Chapters
(433 Verses)

Key Verses:
Romans 1:16, 17

## WRITTEN BY

The Apostle Paul from Corinth where he spent 18 months (Acts 18:11). Paul is the apostle of *FAITH*. Peter is the apostle of *HOPE*. John is the apostle of *LOVE*. James is the apostle of *WORKS*.

## WRITTEN TO

The believers in Rome.

## DATE WRITTEN

Approximately 58 A.D.

## PURPOSE OF BOOK

To explain how sinful man can become right with God by faith in Jesus Christ.

## THEME

The Gospel of Christ which is the power of God to believers.

## BRIEF DESCRIPTION

Paul includes all men as having fallen short of God's

glory on their own merits, regardless of whether they are immoral or moral, Gentiles or Jews. By going back to the examples of Abraham and David, he declares that man becomes right in God's eyes only by faith in Jesus Christ; that Jesus Christ is the answer to the sinful nature of man inherent in him through Adam; and that Jesus Christ paid the penalty for all sins committed by man. Before discussing a Christian's conduct, Paul takes up the subject of Israel's past, present and future relationship to God. Paul relates that only through the power of the Holy Spirit and complete submission to God can a Christian live a life pleasing to God.

## KEY VERSES: ROMANS 1:16, 17

For I am not ashamed of the Gospel of Christ: for it is the power of God unto salvation to every one that believeth; to the Jew first, and also to the Greek. For therein is the righteousness of God revealed from faith to faith: as it is written, The just shall live by faith.

## KEY WORDS

Faith—37 times
Justify (just, justified)—17 times
Christ—39 times

## KEY WORD FOR EACH CHAPTER

1. Gospel
2. Judgment
3. Sinned
4. Abraham
5. Peace
6. Dead
7. Wretched
8. Spirit
9. Past

10. Present (adj.)
11. Future
12. Present (verb)
13. Subject
14. Weak
15. Hope
16. Salute

### OUTLINE

| | |
|---|---|
| Ch. 1-8 | Doctrinal—How the Gospel saves the sinner |
| Ch. 9-11 | National—How the Gospel relates to Israel |
| Ch. 12-16 | Practical—How the Gospel bears on conduct |

### ALTERNATE OUTLINE

| | |
|---|---|
| Ch. 1:1-17 | Introduction |
| Ch. 1:18-3:20 | Plight of Man |
| Ch. 3:21-4:25 | The Gospel is the answer to Sins—Judicially |
| Ch. 5:1-11 | The Gospel is the answer to Sins—Experientially |
| Ch. 5:12-7:6 | The Gospel is the answer to Sin—Judicially |
| Ch. 7:7-8:39 | The Gospel is the answer to Sin—Experientially |
| Ch. 9 | The past relationship of the nation of Israel to God |
| Ch. 10 | The present relationship of the nation of Israel to God |
| Ch. 11 | The future relationship of the nation of Israel to God |
| Ch. 12-16 | The individual believer and how his conduct should relate to the Gospel |

## SPECIAL OUTLINE FOR CHAPTER 12

Ch. 12:1          What the believer's relationship to God should be

Ch. 12:2          What the believer's relationship to the world should be

Ch. 12:3-16       What the believer's relationship to other believers should be

Ch. 12:17-21      What the believer's relationship tot he rest of the world should be

## CHAPTER BY CHAPTER

Ch.   1:1-17 Paul writes of his intent to visit Rome and that he is ready, willing and able to preach the Gospel.

Ch.   1:18-32 All men know that God exists but there are those who are indifferent, idolatrous and immoral.

Ch.   2:1-16 The Gentile who is moral is not good enough in God's eyes.

Ch.   2:17-29 The Jew, to whom the law was given, cannot please God.

Ch.   3 Paul concludes none is righteous, all are under sin, and that only faith in Jesus, apart from the deeds of the law, can save the individual.

Ch.   4 Abraham and David were found righteous in God's eyes upon the basis of faith in God's Word and apart from their deeds.

Ch.   5 Certain benefits accrue to the believer as a result of his faith in Christ.

Ch.   6 A man who becomes a Christian is dead in Christ, freed from the power of sin, and need no longer serve sin.

Ch.   7 Paul states that although a Christian is dead to the law, his old nature is still with him, which creates internal conflict.

Ch. 8 Paul realizes that a Christian can please God only through the power of the Holy Spirit and by being led by Him.

Ch. 9 The past relationship of the nation of Israel to God.

Ch. 10 The present relationship of the nation of Israel to God.

Ch. 11 The future relationship of the nation of Israel to God.

Ch. 12 The believer and what should be his attitude to God, to the world, and to other believers and nonbelievers.

Ch. 13 The believer's relationship, attitude and conduct toward civil authority.

Ch. 14 The believer's relationship, attitude and conduct toward weaker believers.

Ch. 15 What the individual believer's responsibility should be.

Ch. 16 Personal greetings and parting exhortations.

# I CORINTHIANS

16 Chapters                                  Key Verse:
(437 Verses)                      I Corinthians 10:31

## WRITTEN BY

The Apostle Paul from Ephesus (16:7, 8).

## WRITTEN TO

The saints (Gentile Greek believers) sanctified in
Christ Jesus which is the church of God in Corinth
(1:2).

## DATE WRITTEN

56 A.D. during Paul's third missionary journey.

## PURPOSES OF BOOK

Paul had spent 18 months with the Corinthians during his first visit to them (Acts 18:1, 11). During his
third missionary journey while he was in Ephesus,
word came to him of the schism or split in the church
because of human teachers. He writes to correct this
situation as well as to answer questions which the Corinthians had written and asked him. In addition Paul
wrote to defend his apostleship and ministry which
were being attacked by false teachers.

## THEME

Reproving the wrong conduct of believers at Corinth brought about more by carnality rather than heresy.

## BRIEF DESCRIPTION

In chapters 1-6, Paul reproves the Corinthians for the factionalism that prevails in the church; he reproves them for their carnality, the sexual immorality among them and also because they couldn't solve their civil problems among themselves and were taking them to the courts.

Paul then answers questions they had written in a letter to him. He writes concerning marriage; food offered to idols; their behavior at the Lord's Supper; spiritual gifts; the condition of love in which gifts thrive best; that prophesy (teaching) is the best gift; and discusses bodily resurrection from the dead.

## SPECIAL INFORMATION

Now all these things happened unto them for ensamples: and they are written for our admonition, upon whom the ends of the world are come (I Cor. 10:11).

This verse says that there are four reasons for studying the Bible.

1. "Now all these things happened." This refers to actual events which occurred and which are recorded in the Old Testament.

2. "... For ensamples unto us." The Greek word for ensamples is *typos,* from which we get the word "type." The Bible should be read for the typology which we get from it. For instance, the Ark (of the flood in Noah's time: Gen. 7, 8) is a type of Christ; Aaron as High Priest is a type of Christ; Egypt is a type of the world; the Exodus is a type of salvation experience; and Joseph is the highest type of Christ in the Old Testament.

3. "And they are written for our admonition...." The experiences described should serve as a warning to us.

4. "... upon whom the ends of the world are come." The period following Christ's ascension (the Church Age) is the final age of man on earth before Christ's Second Advent.

## KEY VERSE: I CORINTHIANS 10:31

Whether therefore ye eat, or drink, or whatsoever ye do, do all to the glory of God.

## KEY WORDS

Divisions
Contentions

## KEY WORD FOR EACH CHAPTER

1. Contentions
2. Spiritual, Natural
3. Labourers
4. Stewards
5. Fornication (Immorality)
6. Lawsuits
7. Marriage
8. Meat, Idols
9. Self Denial (Authority)
10. Challenge
11. Lord's Supper
12. Gifts
13. Love
14. Prophesy
15. Resurrection
16. Collection, Exhortation

## OUTLINE

Bird's-eye view of First Corinthians

A.   General Outline

I. Reproof (of schisms and scandals) (Ch. 1-6)
II. Replies (concerning problems) (Ch. 7-15)
III. Supplementary—closing (Ch. 16)
B.  Specific Outline
   I. Salutation and Thanksgiving (Ch. 1:1-9)
   II. Concerning conditions in the Corinthian church (Ch. 1:10-16:9)
      1. Concerning *DIVISIONS* and party spirit (Ch. 1:10-4:21)
         (1) Centrality of Christ crucified corrects divisions (Ch. 1:10-31)
         (2) Clarity of Holy Spirit corrects human wisdom (Ch. 2)
         (3) Correct concept of God clarifies Christian service (Ch. 3)
         (4) Conditions of Christ's servants constrain Christian conduct (Ch. 4)
      2. Concerning *SCANDALS* in the Corinthian Church (Ch. 5:1-6:20)
         (1) Impurity (Ch. 5:1-13
         (2) Lawsuits among members (Ch. 6)
      3. Concerning *MARRIAGE* (Ch. 7)
      4. Concerning *CHRISTIAN LIBERTY* (Ch. 8:1-11:1)
      5. Concerning *WOMEN IN CHURCH* (Ch. 11:2-16)
      6. Concerning the *LORD'S SUPPER* (Ch. 11:17-34)
      7. Concerning *SPIRITUAL GIFTS* (Ch. 12:1-14:40)
         (1) Endowment of Gifts (Ch. 12)
         (2) Energy of Gifts (Ch. 13)
         (3) Exercise of Gifts (Ch. 14)
      8. Concerning *GOSPEL* (Ch. 15:1-58)
         (1) Prominence of Resurrection in Gospel 15:1-4

## CHAPTER BY CHAPTER

Ch. 1 After a brief introduction and thanksgiving, Paul discusses divisions and contentions among the Corinthians; he says that he was sent to preach the Gospel, not to baptize, and that the Gospel is God's wisdom, not man's, who in his own wisdom can't understand it.

Ch. 2 The revelation of God is not dependent upon human wisdom: it can only be spiritually discerned.

Ch. 3 Carnality prevents spiritual growth; Jesus Christ is the only foundation; two kinds of service and results from each.

Ch. 4 Men will not judge Christians; Christ alone will judge them; Paul uses himself as an example of humility and patience.

Ch. 5 Immorality rebuked; Paul commands discipline; Christians are to be in the world, not of it.

Ch. 6 Christians are not to air their legal problems in courts of law; the body is God's temple and holy.

Ch. 7 Sexual conduct of a Christian couple; regulations concerning marriage; let each remain where he is called; advice to the unmarried.

Ch. 8 Concerning things offered to idols.

Ch. 9 Paul defends his apostleship; those who preach the Gospel are to live by means of the Gospel; the method and reward of Christian service.

Ch. 10 Israel in the wilderness;erness experiences are examples for our learning; consideration of others in eating and drinking.

Ch. 11 Relationship between a Christian man and woman; abuses rebuked concerning the Lord's Supper; meaning of the Lord's Supper.

Ch. 12 Concerning spiritual gifts and their use.

Ch. 13 The atmosphere in which these gifts thrive— love.

Ch. 14 Prophesy (teaching) is the superior gift; the misuse of the gift of tongues; the regulations concerning spiritual gifts in the local church.

Ch. 15 The resurrection of Christ, the importance of it, and the fact of it; the resurrection body of believers.

Ch. 16 Concerning giving; instructions and personal greetings.

# II CORINTHIANS

13 Chapters
(257 Verses)

Key Verses:
II Corinthians 1:3, 4

## WRITTEN BY
The Apostle Paul, probably from Philippi.

## WRITTEN TO
The believers at Corinth, Greece.

## DATE WRITTEN
58 A.D.

## PURPOSES OF BOOK
To strengthen the Corinthian Christians against the persecutions they encountered; to reassert and defend Paul's apostolic authority; to magnify the gospel of Christ; to challenge the Corinthians to faithful stewardship; and to exalt the person and work of Jesus Christ.

## THEME
Christ is the believer's comfort during trials and pressures and Paul's defense of his apostolic authority.

## BRIEF DESCRIPTION

Paul was in Philippi (Macedonia) hoping to see the Corinthians shortly (II Cor. 12:14; 13:1). He had been in Ephesus and in great danger (II Cor. 1:8). He left to go to Troas where despite his problems he preached the Gospel (II Cor. 2:12) and was expecting Titus. When Titus did not come, Paul left and went to Macedonia where Titus came to him with good news (II Cor. 7:6, 7). In the meantime, false teachers were criticizing and questioning his authority. Paul writes because of his concern that the Corinthians might be too severe with the offender of I Cor. 5 (II Cor. 2:5-11). Secondly, Paul gives encouragement and instructions concerning the offering for the poor saints of Jerusalem (II Cor. 8-9). Further, Paul reasserts and defends his apostolic authority against the false teachers (II Cor. 10:10; 11:4; 12:12; 13:3).

## KEY VERSES: II CORINTHIANS 1:3, 4

Blessed be God, even the Father of our Lord Jesus Christ, the Father of mercies, and the God of all comfort; Who comforteth us in all our tribulation, that we may be able to comfort them which are in any trouble, by the comfort wherewith we ourselves are comforted of God.

## KEY WORDS

Ministry (or variations)—18 times
Reconciliation
Comfort

## KEY WORD FOR EACH CHAPTER

1. Comfort
2. Savior
3. Glory
4. Inward, renewed

60

5. Reconciliation
 6. Separate
 7. Titus
 8. Macedonia
 9. Cheerful giver
10. Authority
11. Godly jealousy
12. Revelations
13. Examine yourselves

## *OUTLINE*

Ch. 1:1-11          Introduction
Ch. 1:12-7:16       Paul's principles of action in his
                    ministry
Ch. 8:1-9:15        Concerning the collection for the
                    poor at Jerusalem
Ch. 10:1-13:10      Paul's defense of his apostolic au-
                    thority
Ch. 13:11-14        Conclusion

## *ALTERNATE OUTLINE*

Ch. 1:1-2           Introduction
Ch. 1:3-5           Paul's account of his ministry
                        a. As to the motive (1-2)
                        b. As to the message (3-5)
Ch. 6-9             Paul's appeal to his converts
                        a. Concerning spiritual things
                           (6-7)
                        b. Concerning material things
                           (8-9)
Ch. 10-13           Paul's answer to his critics
                        a. The critics and their preten-
                           sions (accusations)
                        b. The Apostle and his creden-
                           tials
Ch. 13:11-14        Conclusion

61

## CHAPTER BY CHAPTER

Ch. 1 Paul tells of his suffering; that he has a clear conscience; and that the reason he did not visit the Corinthians was in order to spare them embarrassment.

Ch. 2 Paul appeals for the offender of I Cor. 5:1-11; he preached the Gospel in Troas; was uneasy because Titus did not show up; is thankful to God; and speaks of his sincerity.

Ch. 3 The preaching of the Gospel is much more glorious than the old covenant.

Ch. 4 Paul speaks of his sincerity, the pressures brought to bear against him, and of his faithfulness.

Ch. 5 Paul tells of the ministry of reconciliation and that Christians are ambassadors for Christ.

Ch. 6 Paul appeals to the Corinthians to live separated lives from unbelievers.

Ch. 7 Paul is comforted by the coming of Titus; Paul rejoices for the repentant attitude of the Corinthians.

Ch. 8 Paul appeals to the Corinthians to be generous in their giving started a year previously, and uses the generosity of the Macedonians as an example.

Ch. 9 Paul stresses the benefits derived from giving.

Ch. 10 Paul asserts his apostolic authority.

Ch. 11 Paul gives his reasons for asserting his authority; Paul's suffering for Christ is a further proof of his apostleship.

Ch. 12 The visions and revelations as well as his love for the Corinthians are a further sign of his apostleship.

Ch. 13 Paul warns them that he will manifest his apostolic authority when he comes to them again.

# GALATIANS

6 Chapters                          Key Verse:
(149 Verses)                    Galatians 5:1

### WRITTEN BY
The Apostle Paul from Rome.

### WRITTEN TO
All the believers of Galatia.

### DATE WRITTEN
55 A.D.

### PURPOSES OF BOOK
To refute and combat the teaching of Judaizers who
were saying that even though Christ had given them
salvation they must still keep the law to ensure their
salvation. Written to correct wrong thinking.

### THEME
The liberty which God has given believers in Christ
Jesus and Paul's defense of it.

### BRIEF DESCRIPTION
The Apostle Paul presents his authority to write this
epistle as having come directly from Jesus Christ. He

notes that he did not see any of the Apostles for three years. Fourteen years later when he did bring the Gentile, Titus, with him to see the Apostles, they agreed with him as to Titus' salvation. Paul explains that justification is by faith in Christ alone, apart from the works of the law, by explaining that Christ had died to redeem them from the law. The promise to Abraham, and to all like him, of salvation by faith was made 430 years before the law was given. Paul makes an allegory between the two sons of Abraham, Ishmael, born of a slave, Hagar (Gen. 16), and Isaac, born of Sarah (Gen. 21) and free. Paul gives practical suggestions as to how the Galatians should conduct themselves in view of the freedom they have in Christ.

### SPECIAL INFORMATION
### THE FRUIT OF THE SPIRIT

Love (foundation attitude for) joy, peace (inward attitudes to self)
Longsuffering (foundation attitude for) gentleness, goodness (outward attitudes to man)
Faith (foundation attitude for) meekness, temperance (upward attitudes toward God).

### KEY VERSE: GALATIANS 5:1

Stand fast therefore in the liberty wherewith Christ hath made us free, and be not entangled again with the yoke of bondage.

### KEY WORDS

Free (Freewoman)—7 times
Law—32 times
Faith—21 times

### KEY WORD FOR EACH CHAPTER

1. Gospel
2. Peter

3. Abraham
4. Two Sons
5. Spirit
6. Communicate

## OUTLINE

Ch. 1-2 Personal—
Narrative (about Paul)—Authenticity of Gospel:
Chapter 1—by Origin;
Chapter 2—by Nature; 1-10 Compare—11-21
    Contest
Ch. 3-4 Doctrinal—
Discussion (about Gospel)—Superiority of Gospel over Judaism by relation which it effects
Chapter 3—by relation to Jesus (Sonship)
Chapter 4—by privileges of a son which it gives
    (Privileges)
Ch. 5-6 Practical—
Exhortation (to Galatians)—Liberty of the Gospel
Chapter 5:1-15—Love service ends law bondage
Chapters 5:6-6:10—Spirit ends flesh bondage
Ch. 6:11-18 Postscript

## ALTERNATE OUTLINE

Ch. 1-2    Basis of Liberty—Personal
Ch. 3-4    Truth of Liberty—Doctrinal
Ch. 5-6    True Effect of Liberty—Practical

## CHAPTER BY CHAPTER

Ch. 1:1-5          Salutation: Shortest of Paul's Letters
Ch. 1:6-10         Reason for writing
Ch. 1:11-2:14      Paul declares his authority is from Christ; that he never learned the Gospel from men; this Gospel

# EPHESIANS

6 Chapters
(155 Verses)

Key Verses:
Ephesians 1:22, 23

## WRITTEN BY

The Apostle Paul

## WRITTEN TO

The believers (saints) at Ephesus and to believers in general (1:1).

## DATE WRITTEN

Approximately 64 A.D. from Rome while Paul was in prison.

## PURPOSES OF BOOK

To strengthen the believers in their faith; to encourage them to walk worthy of their position; and to reveal the mystery that believing Jews and Gentiles are members of the body of Christ.

## THEME

The heavenly position God has given to the believer as part of the body of Christ and how the believer should conduct himself in view of that position.

## BRIEF DESCRIPTION

The Apostle Paul describes the spiritual blessings which God has given believers and tells of the heavenly position which they have as joint members of the body of Christ. He also reveals the mystery that believing Jews and Gentiles are members of the body of Christ. He instructs them as to how they should conduct themselves by "putting off the old man" and "putting on the new man." He prepares them for spiritual warfare against the unseen enemy, Satan.

## SPECIAL INFORMATION

*The spiritual blessings which God has blessed us with in heavenly places are:*

1. Election—He has "chosen us before the foundation of the earth." 1:4
2. Predestination—He has "predestinated us unto the adoption of children." 1:5
3. Acceptance—He has "made us to be accepted in the beloved." 1:6
4. Redemption—He has redeemed us. 1:7
5. Revelation—He has revealed the mystery of His will to us. 1:9
6. Inheritance—He has given us an inheritance. 1:11
7. Sealing by the Spirit—He has sealed us to Himself with the Holy Spirit. 1:13

## KEY VERSES: EPHESIANS 1:22, 23

And hath put all things under his feet, and gave him to be the head over all things to the church, Which is his body, the fulness of him that filleth all in all.

## KEY WORDS

In Christ—93 times
Grace—12 times
Body—8 times
Walk—8 times

## KEY WORD FOR EACH CHAPTER

1. Blessings
2. Sit
3. Mystery
4. Walk
5. Spirit
6. Armor

## OUTLINE

Ch. 1, 2, 3   Believer's WEALTH in Christ—Doctrinal

Ch. 4, 5, 6  Believer's WALK in Christ—Practical

## CHAPTER BY CHAPTER

| | |
|---|---|
| Ch. 1:1-14 | Praise for spiritual possessions |
| Ch. 1:15-23 | Prayer for spiritual perception |
| Ch. 2:1-10 | Our new condition in Christ |
| Ch. 2:11-22 | Our new relation in Christ |
| Ch. 3:1-12 | Revealing of the Divine Mystery |
| Ch. 3:13-21 | Receiving of the Divine Fullness |
| Ch. 4:1-16 | Our walk regarding the Church corporately |
| Ch. 4:17-32 | The believer's conduct not as other Gentiles |
| Ch. 5:1-14 | The believer's walk in love and as a child of light |
| Ch. 5:15-21 | The Spirit-filled walk |
| Ch. 5:22-6:9 | Special instructions for wives, husbands, children, father, servants and masters |
| Ch. 6:10-18 | The Christian warfare |
| Ch. 6:19-22 | Paul's personal request for prayer |
| Ch. 6:23-24 | Concluding benediction |

# PHILIPPIANS

4 Chapters                                    Key Verse:
(104 Verses)                          Philippians 2:5

## WRITTEN BY

The Apostle Paul

## WRITTEN TO

The believers (saints) at Philippi, The word "saint" means one who has been set apart by God.

## DATE WRITTEN

Approximately 62 A.D. from Rome while Paul was in prison; delivered by Epaphroditus.

## PURPOSES OF BOOK

The Philippians had sent a gift to Paul by the hand of Epaphroditus (4:18) when he was in prison in Rome. While he was in Rome, Epaphroditus became seriously ill, on the verge of death (2:27). The Philippians were concerned over his illness and Epaphroditus was distressed that they had heard about it, and he longed to see them (2:26). After he recovered, Paul sent him back to the Philippians (2:25).

## THEME

God is all sufficient to be the strength of the believer and to meet his needs; to rejoice in the Lord regardless of the circumstances.

## BRIEF DESCRIPTION

Paul tells the Philippians that in order for them to have unity, joy and peace, Christ must be their life and they must claim the mind of Christ. He warns about Judaizing teachers and encourages them to press forward together to the high calling of God in Christ. He exhorts them to be joyful, not to be anxious, and by prayer and supplication to let their needs be known to God who will supply them and give them peace.

## KEY VERSE: PHILIPPIANS 2:5

Let this mind be in you, which was also in Christ Jesus.

## KEY WORD

Joy (rejoice, rejoicing—18 times

## KEY WORD FOR EACH CHAPTER

1. Live
2. Mind
3. Press
4. Strengtheneth

## OUTLINE

**Christ:**
Within us—Chapter 1
Behind us—Chapter 2
Before us—Chapter 3
Above us—Chapter 4

**Christ is Our:**
LIFE—1:21—Inward look to Christ
MIND—2:5—Backward look to Christ
GOAL—Forward look to Christ
STRENGTH—Upward look to Christ

*ALTERNATE OUTLINE*

Chapters 1, 2—Doctrinal
Chapters 3, 4—Practical

CHAPTER BY CHAPTER

| | |
|---|---|
| Ch. 1:1-2 | Salutation |
| Ch. 1:3-11 | Praise and prayer |
| Ch. 1:12-18 | Progress of the gospel in spite of persecution and false motives |
| Ch. 1:19-26 | Paul's determination that Christ be magnified "by life or by death" |
| Ch. 1:27-30 | Paul's encouragement to "stand fast" |
| Ch. 2:1-11 | Importance of humility |
| Ch. 2:12-18 | God at work in the lives of the believers; Paul's desire for them to have joy in sacrificial service, "holding forth the word of life" |
| Ch. 2:19-24 | Timothy as an example |
| Ch. 2:25-30 | Epaphroditus as an example |
| Ch. 3:1-17 | Paul as an example |
| Ch. 3:18-21 | Friends and enemies of Christ |
| Ch. 4:1-3 | Paul's exhortation for steadfastness and harmony |
| Ch. 4:4-7 | The peace that comes with complete trust in God |
| Ch. 4:8-9 | The peace that comes from pure thoughts |
| Ch. 4:10-12 | The peace of contentment in any state |

# COLOSSIANS

4 Chapters
(95 Verses)

Key Verses:
Colossians 1:18, 2:10

## WRITTEN BY

The Apostle Paul.

## WRITTEN TO

The Church at Colossae.

## DATE WRITTEN

62 A.D. from Rome while Paul was in prison and delivered by Tychicus and Onesimus (4:7-9).

## PURPOSES OF BOOK

Paul had not visited Colossae, but had learned of the church there from Epaphras (1:7) who probably had been in prison with him (Philemon 23). He sent this letter to them by Tychicus (4:7, 8), who was accompanied by Onesimus (4:9) (Philemon 10-12). Paul planned to visit them later (Philemon 22). However, he wrote this letter to the Colossians to warn them against serious errors of doctrine (to correct their wrong thinking, II Tim. 3:16) and to reprove their wrong conduct. Paul wrote:

1. To warn them against human philosophy and to urge them to give Christ the supreme place He rightfully deserves as head of all powers (2:8-10) (1:18).
2. To warn them against Jewish ritualism (2:16). False Judaizing teachers were evidently at work.
3. To warn them against the worship of angels instead of worshipping Christ. (2:18, 19)
4. To warn them against false asceticism (2:20-23). Webster defines asceticism as: "Doctrine that through self-torture or self-denial, one can discipline himself to reach a high state, spiritually or intellectually." The Colossians were placing undue emphasis on human wisdom, ritualism and ordinances. They were not giving Christ the supreme position as head, which He rightly deserved.

## THEME

God's fullness dwells in Jesus Christ who is the head of the church, which is His body, and He is the Creator of the Universe (1:15-19).

## BRIEF DESCRIPTION

Paul identifies the person of Christ as the Creator, the Divine Head of the Universe. He discusses the believer's completeness in Him. As a result of what Christ has done for the believer, the Christian is encouraged to conduct himself accordingly by "putting on the new man" and "putting off the old man."

## SPECIAL INFORMATION

**Christ is all in all:**
His Deity—The image of the invisible God (1:15)
Creation—Sovereign Creator of the universe (1:15-16)
Preeminence—Before all things (1:18)

Redemption—Through his Blood ... to reconcile all things (1:20)
Headship—Over all principalities and powers (1:18, 2:15)
His church—The head of the body (1:18, 2:19)
His Indwelling Presence—The Christian's Hope (1:27)

## The Church's position "in Christ" is:
United in Christ—2:2
Complete in Christ—2:10
Dead in Christ—2:20
Buried with Christ—Rom. 6:4
Risen with Christ—3:1

### *KEY VERSES: COLOSSIANS 1:18, 2:10*
And he is the head of the body, the church: who is the beginning, the firstborn from the dead; that in all things he might have the preeminence. And ye are complete in him, which is the head of all principality and power:

### *KEY WORDS*
Head—3 times
Fullness

### *KEY WORD FOR EACH CHAPTER*
1. Head
2. Fullness
3. Put on
4. Walk, Watch

### *OUTLINE*
Chapter 1, 2—Doctrinal—That ye may be filled.
Chapter 3, 4—Practical—That ye walk worthily.

## CHAPTER BY CHAPTER

| | |
|---|---|
| Ch. 1:1-8 | Introductory thanksgiving |
| Ch. 1:9-14 | Prayer for fullness and walking worthy |
| Ch. 1:15-18 | Christ the fullness of God in creation |
| Ch. 1:19-23 | Christ the fullness of God in redemption |
| Ch. 1:24-29 | Christ the fullness of God in the Church |
| Ch. 2:1-23 | Christ the fullness of God against heresy |
| Ch. 2:1-7 | Warning against being beguiled with enticing words |
| Ch. 2:8-10 | Warning against human wisdom and worldly teachings |
| Ch. 2:11-17 | Warning against empty ritualism |
| Ch. 2:18-19 | Warning against worshipping angels and false mysticism |
| Ch. 2:20-23 | Warning against false ascetism |
| Ch. 3:1-11 | The new life and believers individually |
| Ch. 3:12-17 | Believers' relationship to other believers |
| Ch. 3:18-21 | Family relationships |
| Ch. 3:22-41 | Employment responsibilities |
| Ch. 4:2-6 | Believers' relationship to non-believers |
| Ch. 4:7-18 | Personal remarks, salutations and final instructions |

# I THESSALONIANS

5 Chapters
(89 Verses)

Key Verses:
I Thessalonians 3:5-7

## WRITTEN BY

The Apostle Paul from Corinth. This is the first of Paul's letters recorded in Scripture.

## WRITTEN TO

The Thessalonians of the city of Thessalonica, Greece (See Acts 17:1-9).

## DATE WRITTEN

Approximately 53 A.D. during Paul's second missionary journey.

## PURPOSES OF BOOK

During his second missionary journey, Paul visited Thessalonica. In three weeks' time, as Paul "reasoned with them out of the scriptures," some of the Jewish Thessalonians believed (Acts 17:1-4). Paul was forced to leave and eventually arrived in Athens. There he was worried about the Thessalonians and sent Timothy back to find out how they were. When Timothy returned to Paul with good news, Paul wrote this letter to tell them how he was comforted by their faith. He also wrote to encourage them to stand firm in the face of persecution (2:14) and to maintain sexual purity (4:1-8); to comfort them concerning those who had died (4:13-18); to exhort them to be watchful concerning Christ's return (5:1-11); and to encourage spiritual unity among them.

## THEME
Christ's return is the Christian's hope. Each chapter mentions it: (1:10; 2:12, 19; 3:13; 4:13-18; 5:1-11, 23).

## BRIEF DESCRIPTION
Paul first thanks God for the Thessalonians, reminiscing about how they were saved and what good examples they were to all believers in Greece. He reminds them of his motives for coming to them (1:1-6), of his conduct (1:7-12), of the message he brought, and of his unselfish concern. He tells how he was worried about them and sent Timothy to find out how they were. When Timothy returned with good news, Paul was comforted. Paul gives practical suggestions as to how they should conduct themselves and not slip back into the immorality practiced by unbelievers. He exhorts them to study and to work. He comforts them by telling them how Christ will return for those who know Him as Savior. He admonishes them to live soberly and watchfully, expecting Christ's return at any moment. They are to know and respect those laboring among them who are spiritually stronger in the Lord. He exhorts them to be considerate and to live unblemished lives.

## KEY VERSES: I THESSALONIANS 3:5-7
For this cause, when I could no longer forbear, I sent to know your faith, lest by some means the tempter

have tempted you, and our labour be in vain. But now when Timotheus came from you unto us, and brought us good tidings of your faith and charity, and that ye have good remembrance of us always, desiring greatly to see us, as we also to see you: Therefore, brethren, we were comforted over you in all our affliction and distress by your faith:

## KEY WORDS

Coming (of the Lord)—4 times
Comfort—6 times

### KEY WORD FOR EACH CHAPTER

1. Remembering
2. Entrance
3. Timothy
4. Sleep
5. Thief

## OUTLINE

| | |
|---|---|
| Ch. 1-3 | Remembering: How they were saved, dealt with, and cared for. |
| Ch. 4-5 | How they should live their lives to please God. |

### SPECIAL OUTLINE

| | |
|---|---|
| I Cor. 13:13 | "And now abideth faith, hope, love" |
| Ch. 1:3 | "your work of *faith*" |
| Ch. 1:3 | "labour of *love*" |
| Ch. 1:3 | "patience of *hope*" |
| Ch. 1:9 | "ye turned to God from idols" |
| Ch. 1:9 | "to serve the living and true God" |
| Ch. 1:10 | "to wait for his Son from heaven" |

Because of faith—you turned (in the past)
Because of love—you serve (in the present)
Because of hope—you wait (in the future)

## CHAPTER BY CHAPTER

Ch. 1  Paul *reminisces* concerning their faith, hope and love and what outstanding examples of believers they were.

Ch. 2  Paul *reviews* his motivation in coming to them, his conduct, his message, and his unselfish concern for them.

Ch. 3  Paul tells them he *was relieved* when he received good news concerning their faith from Timothy whom he had sent to them.

Ch. 4  Paul *exhorts* them to live separated lives; *comforts* them by telling them how Christ will return.

Ch. 5  Paul *warns* them as to how Christ will come and to live their lives as though He were to come at any moment.

# II THESSALONIANS

3 Chapters                         Key Verses:
(47 Verses)           II Thessalonians 2:3, 7, 8

## WRITTEN BY

The Apostle Paul from Corinth, approximately three months after he wrote I Thessalonians.

## WRITTEN TO

The believers in Thessalonica.

## DATE WRITTEN

Probably in the Spring of 53 A.D.

## PURPOSES OF BOOK

Paul wrote this second epistle to clear up misunderstandings arising from what he said in his first letter. Because of what he had said there, some of the Thessalonian believers had quit working and were idly waiting for the Lord's return. Some had become troublemakers. Moreover, there was a letter purportedly from Paul which confused them. Paul writes that they "be not soon shaken in mind" (II Thess. 2:2), and reminds them of what he told them while he was with them during his second missionary journey concerning the conditions which will exist upon earth immediately prior to the Lord's return.

## THEME

Christians are to be patiently waiting, watching, and working, up to the very moment of the Lord's return.

## BRIEF DESCRIPTION

In chapter one, after a brief salutation, Paul comforts them during their present tribulation, and encourages them by telling them how, in the future, they will be compensated for their patience. In chapter two, Paul explains the conditions and the circumstances of Christ's return. In chapter three, he gives instructions as to how they should conduct themselves while awaiting the Lord's return.

## KEY VERSES: II THESSALONIANS 2:3, 7, 8

Let no man deceive you by any means: for that day shall not come, except there come a falling away first, and that man of sin be revealed, the son of perdition; For the mystery of iniquity doth already work: only he who now letteth will let, until he be taken out of the way. And then shall that Wicked be revealed, whom the Lord shall consume with the spirit of his mouth, and shall destroy with the brightness of his coming:

## KEY WORDS

Command—4 times
Coming—3 times
Revealed—3 times

## KEY WORD FOR EACH CHAPTER

1. Recompense
2. Day of Christ
3. Command

## OUTLINE

| | |
|---|---|
| Ch. 1:1, 2 | Salutation |
| Ch. 1:3-12 | Comfort from the hope of the Lord's return |
| Ch. 2:1-17 | Information regarding the Lord's return |
| Ch. 3:1-18 | Commandments concerning conduct |

## ALTERNATE OUTLINE

| | |
|---|---|
| Ch. 1 | Encouragement |
| Ch. 2 | Doctrinal |
| Ch. 3 | Practical |

## CHAPTER BY CHAPTER

Ch. 1 Comfort of the hope of Christ's return during present stress (3-7). Compensation by His return in the future (8-12).

Ch. 2 When and how the Lord will return (1-12). Why and how of waiting for His return (13-17).

Ch. 3 Basis of command: Confidence in the Lord (1-5). Basic command: We must work while we wait (6-15).

# I TIMOTHY

6 Chapters                                  Key Verse:
(113 Verses)                        I Timothy 3:15

## *WRITTEN BY*

The Apostle Paul, probably from Laodicea or Macedonia.

## *WRITTEN TO*

Timothy (1:2; 1:18; 6:20). The name Timothy comes from two Greek words *Timo,* to respect or honor, and *Theos,* which means God, i.e., one who respects or honors God.

## *DATE WRITTEN*

Approximately 66-67 A.D., about the same time Titus was written.

## *PURPOSE OF BOOK*

Paul met Timothy on his first missionary journey (Acts 14:6, 7). On Paul's second missionary journey Timothy was circumcised, ordained and left home to travel with Paul (Acts 16:1-3; I Tim. 4:14; II Tim. 1:6). Of all who traveled with Paul, Timothy was his most constant and faithful companion (Phil. 2:19-22).

Timothy was serving a group of believers as their minister. After Paul's release from prison the first time, he wrote Timothy to warn against false teachers and to encourage and "charge" Timothy to "guard" the Gospel; that is, Timothy was exhorted to be strong in sound doctrine, to be an effective teacher, and to be an example of godly behavior. Paul knew he was near the end of his life and apparently thought it wise for Timothy to have in his possession a letter containing a restatement of oral advice which Paul previously had given him (I Tim. 1:3-4), in case Timothy was challenged upon some point.

## THEME

A charge to guard the faith (1:18; 6:13, 20). Administration and conduct in the local church.

## BRIEF DESCRIPTION

Paul first warns Timothy against unsound doctrine; gives a brief testimony; and exhorts Timothy to conduct himself as a "good minister of Jesus Christ." He advises how the church should be organized; what the public prayer life of men in the church should be; and how some women should conduct themselves. He gives the qualifications for bishops and deacons. Timothy is warned concerning apostasy (falling away) in the church, and to guard against it by being a "good minister of Jesus Christ" through sound teaching and exemplary conduct. Paul discusses what Timothy's relationship as a minister should be to different groups in the church, such as widows, elders, servants and the wealthy.

## KEY VERSE: I TIMOTHY 3:15

But if I tarry long, that thou mayest know how thou oughtest to behave thyself in the house of God, which is the church of the living God, the pillar and ground of the truth.

## KEY WORDS

"Good Minister"—1 time
Doctrine—8 times
Godliness—8 times
Teach, teacher—7 times
Good—22 times

## KEY WORD FOR EACH CHAPTER

1. Charge
2. Prayers
3. Bishop, Deacons
4. Depart
5. Elder, Widow
6. Servants, Rich

## OUTLINE

I. The Faith of the Church—Ch. 1
   a. Introduction (1-2)
   b. Warning against unsound doctrine (3-10)
   c. Personal Testimony of Paul (11-17)
   d. Charge to Timothy (18-20)
II. The Church and Its Conduct—Ch. 2-3
   a. Concerning Order—Ch. 2
      1. Public prayer (1-7)
      2. How men are to pray (8)
      3. Women and their conduct (9-15)
   b. Concerning Office—Ch. 3
      1. Qualifications of elders (1-7)
      2. Qualifications of deacons (8-14)
III. The Minister and His Conduct—Ch. 4-6
   a. To the Church in General—Ch. 4
      1. A "good minister" in faithful teaching (1-11)

2. A "good minister" in exemplary living (12-16)
   b.  Toward Particular Classes—Ch. 5, 6
      1. To older and younger (1, 2)
      2. To widows (3-16)
      3. To elders (17-25)
      4. To servants (6:1-8)
      5. To the rich (9-19)
      6. Closing appeal (20-21)

## CHAPTER BY CHAPTER

Ch. 1 Paul warns against false teaching, gives a brief testimony, and charges Timothy to guard against faithlessness.

Ch. 2 How men should pray in public, and how women should conduct themselves in public.

Ch. 3 The qualifications of bishops and deacons.

Ch. 4 Warning against apostasy and how to guard against it by sound teaching and exemplary behavior.

Ch. 5 Relationship of Timothy (minister) to widows and elders.

Ch. 6 Relationship of Timothy (minister) to servants and rich.

# II TIMOTHY

4 Chapters
(83 Verses)

Key Verses:
II Timothy 4:1-5

## WRITTEN BY

The Apostle Paul, from prison in Rome.

## WRITTEN TO

Timothy.

## DATE WRITTEN

67 A.D.

## PURPOSES OF BOOK

Paul's purpose in writing was to challenge and encourage Timothy to boldness and faithfulness in the face of present testings; to warn him of the apostasy in the future; and to tell Timothy to come to see him as quickly as possible, bringing certain cherished possessions (1:4, 4:9, 13, 21).

## THEME

A challenge to endure pressures and afflictions in the face of apostasy and to be strong in the faith.

## BRIEF DESCRIPTION

Paul exhorts Timothy not to be afraid or ashamed. By using examples of a soldier, an athlete and a farmer, Paul challenges and encourages Timothy to study, to apply himself in his testimony, and to lead a pure, separated and disciplined life. Paul warns Timothy of the apostasy of the last days, and that his resources to stand firm are the "holy scriptures." Paul charges and challenges Timothy to be bold in his testimony in words and deeds, and to endure. He tells Timothy that with his confidence in the Lord, he is ready to die and he asks Timothy to come to see him before winter, bringing needed possessions.

## KEY VERSES: II TIMOTHY 4:1-5

I charge thee therefore before God, and the Lord Jesus Christ, who shall judge the quick and the dead at his appearing and his kingdom: Preach the word; be instant in season, out of season; reprove, rebuke, exhort with all longsuffering and doctrine. For the time will come then they will not endure sound doctrine; but after their own lusts shall they heap to themselves teachers, having itching ears: And they shall turn away their ears from the truth, and shall be turned unto fables. But watch thou in all things, endure afflictions, do the work of an evangelist, make full proof of thy ministry.

## SPECIAL INFORMATION

I and II Timothy were among Paul's final writings; II Timothy was his last epistle. Since he was in prison and ready to die, this "deathbed" testament sets forth his last attitudes, his last thoughts, and his last advice.

He states:

1. Be an example of believers—I Tim. 4:12

2. Neglect not the gift (energy or spiritual talent)—I Tim. 4:14
3. Take heed unto thyself and doctrines—I Tim. 4:16
4. Fight the good fight of faith—I Tim. 6:12
5. Stir up the gift of God—II Tim. 1:6
6. Be not ashamed—II Tim. 1:8
7. Commit thou—II Tim. 2:2
8. Endure hardness—II Tim. 2:3
9. Charge them—II Tim. 2:14
10. Study to show thyself approved—II Tim. 2:15
11. Shun profane and vain babbling—II Tim. 2:16
12. Purge yourself from vessels of dishonor—II Tim. 2:21
13. Flee youthful lusts—II Tim. 2:22
14. Avoid foolish questions—II Tim. 2:23
15. Be gentle, apt to teach, patient—II Tim. 2:24
16. Continue thou ... in the scriptures—II Tim. 3:14, 15
17. Preach the word ... —II Tim. 4:2
18. Endure ... do the work of an evangelist—II Tim. 4:5

## KEY WORDS

Suffer—5 times
Good—5 times
Endure—4 times

## KEY WORD FOR EACH CHAPTER

1. Stir
2. Strong, Commit
3. Scriptures
4. Charge, Watch

## OUTLINE

Salutation 1:1, 2
The True Pastor and Present Testings—Ch. 1, 2

(Internal Attitude) The True Personal Reaction 1:3-2:13

*Challenge*—"stir up" (1:6), "be not ashamed" (1:8), "be strong" (2:1), "endure" (2:3)

*Incentive*—"remember" (1:6, 2:8), Paul's "example" (1:12, 2:9)

(External Attitude) The True Pastoral Reaction 2:14-26

*Challenge*—"charge" (2:14), "study" (2:15), "shun" (2:16)

*Incentive*—"foundation sure" (2:19, "avoid" (2:23), "souls rescued" (2:26)

The True Pastor and the Last Days—Ch. 3, 4

The True Personal Reaction, Ch. 3

*Challenge*—"perilous times" (3:1-9), "continue thou" (3:14)

*Incentive*—Paul's "example" (3:10, 11), "scripture" (3:15, 16)

The True Pastoral Reaction, Ch. 4

*Challenge*—"preach the word" (4:2), "do the work of an evangelist" (4:5)

*Incentive*—"the coming kingdom" (4:1), "the coming crown" (4:8)

## CHAPTER BY CHAPTER

Ch. 1 After a brief introduction and thanksgiving, Paul exhorts Timothy to "stir up the gift of God" (to flex his spiritual muscles), and not to be afraid or ashamed. He uses himself as an example; then he tells of those who turned away from him, except Onesiphorus.

Ch. 2 Timothy is exhorted to be strong, to endure, to strive, to study, to shun, to flee, to teach.

Ch. 3 A description is given of the dangerous times in the last days; that a Christian's resources are the scriptures.

94

Ch. 4 Paul's final charge to Timothy to preach, to endure; Paul is ready to die; Paul tells Timothy to come to see him before winter.

# TITUS

3 Chapters                   Key Verses:
(46 Verses)            Titus 2:14, 3:8

## WRITTEN BY
The Apostle Paul.

## WRITTEN TO
Titus, a Gentile Greek (Gal. 2:3).

## DATE WRITTEN
Approximately 66-67 A.D., about the same time I Timothy was written.

## PURPOSES OF BOOK
Paul had left Titus on the island of Crete in the Mediterranean Sea to finish his work establishing and organizing churches there (1:5). Paul gives Titus instructions as to the qualifications for elders in the churches, warns against false teachers, and seeks to fortify Titus in his work so that Titus will illustrate the life which believers should live.

## THEME
A sound faith and good works must blend. Good works are evidence of a sound faith.

## BRIEF DESCRIPTION

Paul gives Titus specific instructions as to the kind of men who are qualified to be elders and warns Titus against false teachers. Paul gives Titus instructions as to how various classes of people in the churches should conduct themselves. Paul exhorts Titus to stress to the members they should be careful to maintain good works. He warns against heretics.

## KEY VERSES: TITUS 2:14, 3:8

Who gave himself for us, that he might redeem us from all iniquity, and purify unto himself a peculiar people, zealous of good works. This is a faithful saying, and these things I will that thou affirm constantly, that they which have believed in God might be careful to maintain good works. These things are good and profitable unto men.

## KEY WORDS

Good Works—6 times

## KEY WORD FOR EACH CHAPTER

1. Subvert
2. Sound
3. Maintain

## OUTLINE

1. Introduction (1:1-4)
2. Qualifications for Elders (1:5-9)
3. Warning Against False Teachers (1:10-16)
4. Instructions for Various Classes in the Church (2:1-15)
5. Instructions for Members in General (3:1-11)
6. Conclusion (3:12-15)

## CHAPTER BY CHAPTER

Ch. 1  Salutation (1-4); Qualification of elders (5:9); Warning against false teachers (10-16).

Ch. 2  Instructions for various classes in the church; for old men (1-2); for old women (3); for young women (4-5); for young men (6-8); for servants (9-10); basis for such instructions (11-15).

Ch. 3  General instructions for all (1-11); conclusion (12-15).

# PHILEMON

1 Chapter                       Key Verses:
(25 Verses)              Philemon 10 and 17

### WRITTEN BY
The Apostle Paul (1:1, 19).

### WRITTEN TO
Philemon, a wealthy Greek Christian land and slave-owner at Colossae (1, 2, 10, and Col. 4:9).

### DATE WRITTEN
62 A.D., during Paul's first imprisonment in Rome.

### PURPOSE OF BOOK
Onesimus, a slave of Philemon, probably stole from his owner and then ran away. In his travels he met Paul in Rome who converted him to Christ. Paul then sent him back to Philemon with Tychicus, carrying this letter in which he was interceding and pleading for Onesimus.

### THEME
Paul intercedes with Philemon for Onesimus, a runaway slave.

## BRIEF DESCRIPTION

Paul pleads on behalf of the runaway slave Onesimus.

## SPECIAL INFORMATION

The book also serves as a type of salvation story in which Philemon is a type for God and Paul is a type for Christ pleading, "put that on mine account" (verse 18), even as Christ paid for our sins. The outline for this typology is as follows:

Verses 1-7      Philemon—God
Verses 8-17     Onesimus—Man (Adam)
Verses 18-22    Paul—Jesus Christ

## KEY VERSES: PHILEMON 10 AND 17

I beseech thee for my son Onesimus, whom I have begotten in my bonds: If thou count me therefore a partner, receive him as myself.

## OUTLINE

Verses 1-3       Greeting
Verses 4-8       Paul's Praise of Philemon
Verses 9-17      Paul's Plea for Onesimus
Verses 18-22     Paul's Pledge
Verses 23-25     Salute

## PRACTICAL APPLICATIONS

Life in Christ changes every relationship.

Our relationships to others test our relationship to Christ.

Social evils (slavery, in this case) can be changed by transformed lives.

The request which Paul made of Philemon to accept Onesimus could only have been made to a spiritually mature believer.

# HEBREWS

13 Chapters                                          Key Verse:
(303 Verses)                                      Hebrews 4:14

### WRITTEN BY
Uncertain; possibly the Apostle Paul.

### WRITTEN TO
A particular group of Jewish Christians (13:7, 17-19,
22-24), personally known by the writer, (5:11, 12; 6:9,
10; 10:32-34; 12:4) who had made a profession of
faith in Jesus Christ as Savior (3:1; 4:14; 10:23) and
had given some evidence of being saved (6:10;
10:32-34). However, they tended to look backward to
the old covenant (1:1; 3:5, 6; 7:11; 8:7), were carnal,
spiritually dull, and sluggish (3:12; 5:11-14; 12:25).

### DATE WRITTEN
Probably between 64-67 A.D., and definitely before
the fall of Jerusalem in 70 A.D.

### PURPOSES OF BOOK
To show the relationship of Jesus Christ to the ordinances of God, the sacrificial offerings, the priesthood, and the temple. The book of Hebrews is the

only book which gives a revelation of Jesus Christ's heavenly priesthood and intercessory ministry. Hebrews presents Jesus Christ as the full and final revelation of God. It depicts Jesus Christ's superiority over all previous revelations of God; it shows the superiority of the new covenant over the old covenant; it shows how Jesus Christ fulfills and supercedes the Levitical priesthood and sacrifices. The superiority of Jesus Christ and the new covenant in His blood are used to encourage the Jewish Christian believers to whom the letter was written, and to warn them against apostasy.

## THEME
The priesthood of Jesus Christ.

## BRIEF DESCRIPTION
The author, after identifying the Lord Jesus Christ as the full and final revelation of God and His express image, describes Him as better than any created beings, whether angels or persons, including Moses, Joshua and Aaron. A description shows that the new covenant is better than the old covenant and that Jesus Christ completely fulfills and supercedes the Levitical priesthood and system.

## SPECIAL INFORMATION
### EIGHT WARNINGS ARE GIVEN

| | |
|---|---|
| Ch. 2:1-4 | "give the more earnest heed ... lest" |
| Ch. 3:7-19 | "Harden not your hearts" |
| Ch. 4:1-10 | "Let us therefore fear, lest" |
| Ch. 4:11-13 | "Let us labour ... to enter into that rest, lest" |
| Ch. 5:11-6:20 | "seeing you are dull of hearing ... you have need that one teach you |

|              |                                                                              |
|--------------|------------------------------------------------------------------------------|
|              | again ... let us go on to maturity"                                          |
| Ch. 10:26-31 | "For if we sin willfully ... there remaineth no more sacrifice for sins."   |
| Ch. 12:25-29 | "For if they escaped not ... much more shall not we escape, if we turn away from him." |
| Ch. 13:9-15  | "Be not carried about with divers and strange doctrines."                   |

## *KEY VERSE: HEBREWS 4:14*

Seeing then that we have a great high priest that is passed into the heavens, Jesus the Son of God, let us hold fast our profession.

## *KEY WORDS*

Better—13 times
Perfect—(used in one form or another)—14 times
Eternal, forever—15 times
Partakers—9 times
Heaven, heavenly—17 times

## *KEY WORD FOR EACH CHAPTER*

1. Better
2. Lower
3. Moses
4. Rest
5. Aaron
6. Go on
7. Melchisedec
8. New Covenant
9. Mediator
10. Sacrifice
11. Faith
12. Chastening
13. Conversation

## OUTLINE

I. JESUS—THE NEW AND "BETTER" DELIVERER 1-7
- a. Jesus the God-man—better than Angels. Ch. 1-2
- b. Jesus the new apostle—better than Moses. Ch. 3
- c. Jesus the new leader—better than Joshua. Ch. 4:1-13
- d. Jesus the new priest—better than Aaron. Ch. 4:14-6:20
- e. Jesus the priest after the order of Melchisedec. Ch. 7

II. CALVARY—THE NEW AND "BETTER" COVENANT. 8-10:18
- a. New Covenant has better promises. Ch. 8:6-13
- b. It opens up a better sanctuary. Ch. 9:1-14
- c. It is sealed by a better sacrifice. Ch. 9:15-28
- d. It achieves far better results. Ch. 10:1-18

III. FAITH—THE TRUE AND "BETTER" PRINCIPLE 10:19-13
- a. Faith the true response to these "better" things. Ch. 10:19-39
- b. It has always been vindicated as such: examples. Ch. 11
- c. Is now to endure, patiently looking to Jesus. Ch. 12:1-13
- d. Is to express itself in practical sanctity. Ch. 12:14-13:21

Parting Words 13:22-25

## ALTERNATE OUTLINE

I. Introduction. Ch. 1:1-3
II. Christ as a person superior to all other persons. Ch. 1:4-4:16

III. The preeminence and finality of the priesthood
   of Christ. Ch. 5:1-10:18
IV. The life of faith. Ch. 10:19-13:19
 V. Conclusion. Ch. 13:20-25.


*SECOND ALTERNATE OUTLINE*
                Prologue. Ch. 1:1-4
DOCTRINAL:      Chapter 1:10-18
                Christ and other personalities.
                Ch. 1-7
                Christ and the institutions.
                Ch. 8-10:18
EXHORTATION:Chapter 10:19-39
                To freedom and fellowship.
                Ch. 10:19-25
                To patience and perseverance.
                Ch. 10:32-39
PRACTICAL:      Chapter 11:13-21
                Work of faith. Ch. 11
                Patience of hope. Ch. 12:1-24
                Labor of love. Ch. 13:1-21
                Epilogue. Ch. 13:22-25

*CHAPTER BY CHAPTER*

Ch.   1 Jesus Christ is the express image of God and
        is better than the angels.
Ch.   2 Jesus Christ was made lower than the angels.
Ch.   3 Jesus Christ as "the Apostle" is better than
        Moses.
Ch.   4 Jesus Christ as the new leader is better than
        Moses.
Ch.   5 Jesus Christ as the new High Priest is better
        than Aaron.
Ch.   6 Warning to grow in knowledge and exhorta-
        tion to "be not slothful"
Ch.   7 Melchisedec and Jesus Christ.

# JAMES

5 Chapters                          Key Verses:
(108 Verses)                   James 1:22, 2:20

## WRITTEN BY

James, the half brother of the Lord Jesus Christ
(Matt. 13:55; Gal. 1:19). James is the Apostle of
*WORKS*. Peter is the Apostle of *HOPE*. Paul is the
Apostle of *FAITH*. John is the Apostle of *LOVE*.

## WRITTEN TO

The 12 tribes scattered outside Palestine.

## DATE WRITTEN

45 A.D., approximately 15 years after Jesus Christ's
death on the cross.

## PURPOSE OF BOOK

The first Christians were Jews, and, at first they did
not intend to turn from Judaism but only to purify it.
However, the Christian Jews were suffering persecution and tribulation. As a result, they did not demonstrate their faith in Jesus Christ. James encourages and exhorts them to demonstrate their faith by
their deeds. He states that good works are the result
of faith in Jesus Christ.

## THEME

The faith that justifies a believer will result in his improved moral ethics and practical conduct which will glorify the Lord Jesus Christ.

## BRIEF DESCRIPTION

James does not have a major theme to unify his letter, but moves from one subject to another. He starts by discussing the temptations and trials of the readers and exhorts them to patience. He discusses wealth and its relation to the origin and course of temptation. He writes of hearing and doing the word. He discusses preferential treatment of the rich. He shows that faith is demonstrated by works by using the examples of Abraham and Rahab from the Old Testament. In Chapter three he discusses the damage a man can do with his tongue. In Chapter four he shows the cause of evil, pride, and the remedy for it, humility towards God. In Chapter five he warns the unlawfully rich concerning their future; exhorts the readers to patience; and discusses the taking of oaths; the afflicted; the sick; and prayer. He uses examples from the Old Testament. He closes with an exhortation for the readers to help other Christians when they err from the truth. The book of James has been described as the "Proverbs" of the New Testament.

## KEY VERSES: JAMES 1:22, 2:20

But be ye doers of the word, and not hearers only, deceiving your own selves. But wilt thou know, O vain man, that faith without works is dead?

## SPECIAL INFORMATION
## WHAT TO DO WITH THE WORD OF GOD

Receive it—1:21
Hear it—1:22

Do it—1:23
Examine it—1:25

## KEY WORDS

Faith—16 times
Works—15 times

## KEY WORD FOR EACH CHAPTER

1. Temptations
2. Partial
3. Tongue
4. Proud
5. Rich

## OUTLINE

| | |
|---|---|
| Ch. 1:1 | Introduction |
| Ch. 1:2-15 | The believer and his trials |
| Ch. 1:16-27 | The practice of the truth |
| Ch. 2:1-13 | Impartial treatment of people |
| Ch. 2:14-26 | The relationship of works and faith |
| Ch. 3:1-18 | The control of the tongue |
| Ch. 4:1-12 | The real cause and cure of evil |
| Ch. 4:13-5:11 | The uncertainty and discipline of life |
| Ch. 5:12-20 | Concerning oaths, prayer, erring from truth |

## ALTERNATE OUTLINE

| | |
|---|---|
| Ch. 1:1-21 | Faith the victor of temptation |
| Ch. 1:22-2:26 | Faith demonstrated by action |
| Ch. 3:1-18 | Faith demonstrated by words |
| Ch. 4:1-17 | Faith demonstrated by purity of character |
| Ch. 5:1-20 | Faith demonstrated by conduct and prayer |

## CHAPTER BY CHAPTER

Ch. 1:1  Introduction

Ch. 1:2-15  The believer and his trials

Ch. 1:2-12  Testings from without

Ch. 1:13-15  Temptations from within

Ch. 1:16-27  Be doers as well as hearers of the word

Ch. 2:1-20  Treatment of classes of people contrasted.

Ch. 2:21-26  Examples of good works from the Old Testament.

Ch. 3:1-18  The use of the tongue and how it compares to the governor of a ship, a fire, a fountain; the evidence of wisdom.

Ch. 4:1-17  The cause and remedy for evil; the uncertainty and discipline of life

Ch. 5:1-20  The unlawfully rich are warned; oaths, the afflicted; the sick; prayer; helping another believer to not err from the truth.

# I PETER

5 Chapters                                       Key Verses:
(105 Verses)                                   I Peter 2:9-11

## WRITTEN BY

Peter, probably from Ephesus (I Pet. 5:13). Peter is
the Apostle of *HOPE*. Paul is the Apostle of *FAITH*.
John is the Apostle of *LOVE*. James is the Apostle of
*WORKS*.

## WRITTEN TO

Hebrew Christians ("sojourners of the dispersion") in
Asia Minor (I Pet. 1:1).

## DATE WRITTEN

Approximately 63-64 A.D.

## PURPOSES OF BOOK

Ever since the 10 northern tribes were taken into cap-
tivity in 722 B.C. and the two southern tribes in 586
B.C., the Jews had been scattered geographically.
With the capture of Jerusalem by the troops of the
Roman General Titus in 70 A.D., the nation's future,
including preservation of their national identity, was
doubtful. Many had become Christians in recent

years and since their conversion were suffering great trials and temptations. Peter's two letters were written to strengthen, comfort and encourage these Hebrew believers during their acute trials and sufferings; to brighten their hope; and to exhort them to obedience and patience.

## THEME

Christ is the believer's hope and example during physical and spiritual suffering.

## BRIEF DESCRIPTION

Peter seeks to accomplish his purpose of strengthening, comforting and encouraging, first by showing that the Christian's vocation is salvation and that the living hope he has is the "inheritance incorruptible ... reserved in heaven for you" (1:3-2:10). Peter notes that the behavior of the Christian is characterized by submission in all relationships, whether civil, social or marital (2:11-3:12). Peter explains that the discipline of the Christian is to be accomplished by suffering (3:13-5:11). Christ is depicted as the example of suffering and as the mighty Savior, victorious in suffering.

## KEY VERSES: I PETER 2:9-11

But ye are a chosen generation, a royal priesthood, an holy nation, a peculiar people; that ye should shew forth the praises of him who hath called you out of darkness into his marvellous light: Which in time past were not a people, but are now the people of God: which had not obtained mercy, but now have obtained mercy. Dearly beloved, I beseech you as strangers and pilgrims, abstain from fleshly lusts, which war against the soul.

## KEY WORDS

Suffer—15 plus 6 implied times
Glory, Glorify—16 times
Grace—10 times
Precious—5 times
Hope—4 times

## KEY WORD FOR EACH CHAPTER

1. Salvation
2. Stone
3. One mind
4. Fiery trial
5. Elders

## OUTLINE

| | |
|---|---|
| Ch. 1:1-2 | ADDRESS |
| Ch. 1:3-2:10 | *THE LIVING HOPE–AND WHAT GOES WITH IT*<br>The "living hope" (1:3-12) and our reaction to it (1:13-21)<br>The "living word" (1:22-2:5) and our reaction to it (2:1-3)<br>The "living stone" (2:4) and our relation to it (2:5-10) |
| Ch. 2:11-4:11 | *THE PILGRIM LIFE–AND HOW TO LIVE IT*<br>As citizens (2:12-17), servants (2:18-25), married (3:1-7)<br>As regards outsiders, and enduring suffering (3:8-4:6)<br>As regards other believers, and mutual service (4:7-11) |
| Ch. 4:12-5:11 | *THE "FIERY TRIAL"–AND HOW TO BEAR IT*<br>"Rejoice" and "commit"; the Lord's return near (4:12-19) |

In view of His return elders are to
be examples. (4:1-4)
All are to be humble and vigilant;
glory beyond (5:5-11)

Ch. 5:12-14          FAREWELL

## CHAPTER BY CHAPTER

Ch. 1 Salvation is the hope of the future (1:3-5); the
joy of the present (1:6-9); the theme of the
past (1:10-12). As a result Christians are to be
hopeful and obedient.

Ch. 2 The individual believer is to grow by studying
the word of God (2:1-3); Christians are small
stones as parts of a building (2:4-10); the
conduct of Christians as citizens (2:11-17)
and as servants (2:18-25) is discussed.

Ch. 3 The husband and wife relationship (3:1-7);
conduct in relationship to others (3:8-12);
how a Christian is disciplined by suffering
(3:13-22), with Christ as an example.

Ch. 4 The example of Christ's suffering is continued
(4:1-6); mutual service and relationship
among believers (4:7-11); rejoice concerning
the "fiery trial"; let conduct be above re-
proach (4:12-19).

Ch. 5 Exhorting the elders to be good examples,
humble, vigilant.

# II PETER

3 Chapters
(61 Verses)

Key Verses:
II Peter 2:1, 3:18

## WRITTEN BY

Peter.

## WRITTEN TO

Hebrew Christians scattered in Asia Minor (II Pet. 3:1).

## DATE WRITTEN

Approximately 64 A.D.

## PURPOSES OF BOOK

In Peter's first letter, he was writing to encourage the recipients and to hearten them amid persecution and suffering. He has learned that false teachers among them were teaching false doctrine, so he sent this short letter to remind and to reemphasize to the readers to ground themselves more firmly in the full knowledge of truth in Christ Jesus, and thereby to reinforce their faith against false doctrine.

## THEME

Grow in grace and in the knowledge of Jesus Christ.

Live in the hope of His return.

## BRIEF DESCRIPTION

Knowing that he is going to die, Peter exhorts the Christians to spiritual growth. He warns them of the false teachers, the havoc they are creating, the excesses to which they go, and the peril which they present. Peter warns against scoffers. Peter reminds them that the last days are at hand and that, regardless of the scoffers, the Lord will come in His time; he concludes with the admonition as prophesied that they should live their lives looking for Jesus Christ's return.

## SPECIAL INFORMATION
## COMPARISON WITH II TIMOTHY

1. Both letters were written when the writers knew their lives were nearing an end (II Pet. 1:14 and II Tim. 4:6).
2. Both express deep confidence in the Lord and assurance of the writers' position with Him (II Pet. 1:15, 16 and II Tim. 4:7, 8).
3. Both deal with apostasy, expecially in the "last days" (II Pet. 3:3-5, II Tim. 3:1-5 and II Tim. 4:3).
4. Both exhort their readers to be strong in knowledge and in doctrine (II Pet. 3:18, II Tim. 2:15, II Pet. 1:2 and II Tim. 3:14-17).

## KEY VERSES: II PETER 2:1, 3:18

But there were false prophets also among the people, even as there shall be false teachers among you, who privily shall bring in damnable heresies, even denying the Lord that bought them, and bring upon themselves swift destruction. But grow in grace, and in the knowledge of our Lord and Savior Jesus Christ. To him be glory both now and forever. Amen.

## KEY WORDS

Knowledge (antidote to false teaching)—6 times
Grow

## KEY WORD FOR EACH CHAPTER

1. Promises
2. False prophets
3. Scoffers

## OUTLINE

Ch. 1:1  ADDRESS

Ch. 1  THE KNOWLEDGE OF GOD, AND CHRISTIAN GROWTH
    1. How "these things" are to "abound" (2-11)
    2. Why "these things" are to be "remembered" (12-21)

Ch. 2  THE KNOWLEDGE OF GOD, AND FALSE TEACHERS
    1. The havoc they cause and their destruction (1-9)
    2. Their excesses and the peril they are to believers (10-22)

Ch. 3  THE KNOWLEDGE OF GOD, AND CHRIST'S COMING
    1. The promise upheld against scoffers (1-9)
    2. The promise is a challenge to believers (10-18)

## ALTERNATE OUTLINE

Ch. 1  THE FAITHFUL SHEPHERD FEEDS THE SHEEP
(See John 21:15-16)

Ch. 2-3  THE FAITHFUL SHEPHERD TENDS THE SHEEP
    1. Warning against false teachers (2)

2. Warning against scoffers in the last days (3:8-24)
3. Exhortation to holiness of life in view of Christ's return (3:1-7)

## CHAPTER BY CHAPTER

1. Exhortation to spiritual growth; Peter's impending death; Peter's faithfulness in declaring Christ.
2. The false teachers; their sinful practices and eventual destruction, even as the unrighteous of an earlier period were destroyed.
3. The Second Coming of Christ; His long-suffering; the new heavens and new earth; believers should live expecting His return momentarily.

# I JOHN

5 Chapters
(105 Verses)

Key Verses:
I John 5:11-13

### WRITTEN BY

John the Apostle, probably from Ephesus. John is the Apostle of *LOVE*. Peter is the Apostle of *HOPE*. Paul is the Apostle of *FAITH*. James is the Apostle of *WORKS*.

### WRITTEN TO

Hebrew Christian believers: probably a circular letter.

### DATE WRITTEN

Approximately 90 A.D.

### PURPOSES OF BOOK

To give assurance to those who have eternal life; to encourage and show them how to walk in fellowship with Christ that they "sin not," and that their "joy may be full."

### THEME

How to know the truth and abide in it; how to "have fellowship that your joy may be full" (I John 1:3, 4).

## BRIEF DESCRIPTION

John writes to give assurance of salvation; to warn against error; to encourage the believer to walk in the light; to promote fellowship with God and with other believers; to increase the joy of the believer; and to extend the knowledge of God on the part of the believer.

## SPECIAL INFORMATION
### REASONS WHY I JOHN WAS WRITTEN

| | |
|---|---|
| Ch. 1:3 | "that ye also may have fellowship with us" |
| Ch. 1:4 | "that your joy may be full" |
| Ch. 2:1 | "that ye sin not. And if any man sin, we have an advocate" |
| Ch. 2:13-17 | "I write unto you" |
| | "because ye have known him" |
| | "because ye have overcome" |
| | "because ye are strong" |
| Ch. 2:21-24 | "because ye know the truth" |
| Ch. 2:26 | "concerning them that seduce you" |
| Ch. 5:13 | "that ye may know that ye have eternal life" |

## KEY VERSES: I JOHN 5:11-13

And this is the record, that God hath given to us eternal life, and this life is in his Son. He that hath the Son hath life; and he that hath not the Son of God hath not life. These things have I written unto you that believe on the name of the Son of God; that ye may know that ye have eternal life, and that ye may believe on the name of the Son of God.

## KEY WORD

Know—approximately 35 times

## KEY WORD FOR EACH CHAPTER

1. Light
2. Write
3. Love
4. Try
5. Know

## OUTLINE

| | |
|---|---|
| Ch. 1, 2 | God is Light. |
| Ch. 3, 4 | God is Love. |
| Ch. 5 | God is Life. |

## ALTERNATE OUTLINE

*These are tests of:*

*Profession*—Ch. 1:5-2:11—Light versus darkness.

*Desire*—Ch. 2:12-2:17—Father versus world.

*Doctrine*—Ch. 2:18-2:28—Christ versus antichrist.

*Conduct*—Ch. 2:29-3:24—Good works versus evil works.

*Discernment*—Ch. 4:1-4:6—Holy Spirit versus error.

*Motive*—Ch. 4:7-4:21—Love versus pious pretence.

*New Birth*—Ch. 5:1-5:21—Those that have the Son versus those that have not the son.

## CHAPTER BY CHAPTER

| | |
|---|---|
| Ch. 1:1-4 | Introduction. |
| Ch. 1:5-2:29 | Walking in the light. |
| Ch. 2:1-11 | Christ our Advocate. |
| Ch. 2:12-17 | The family of God. |
| Ch. 2:18-29 | Christ versus antichrist. |
| Ch. 3:1-3 | Be prepared for His coming. |
| Ch. 3:4-12 | Children of God versus children of the devil. |
| Ch. 3:13-24 | Life in fellowship with God and other believers. |

123

# II JOHN

1 Chapter                Key Verse:
(13 Verses)          II John 7, 9, 10

### WRITTEN BY
John the Apostle, from Ephesus.

### WRITTEN TO
A Christian mother and her children.

### DATE WRITTEN
Approximately 95-98 A.D.

### PURPOSES OF BOOK
To give this mother a good report concerning her children (verse 4). Also, there were seducing, deceiving teachers who said and taught that Christ had not and could not come in the flesh. John warns against such people, telling how to avoid being deceived (verse 9), and how to treat deceivers (verses 10, 11).

### THEME
Walk in truth and love; be vigilant against false teaching.

### BRIEF DESCRIPTION
After a short greeting, John exhorts the mother to

walk in the truth as she had received it. He states that anyone who teaches that Christ has not come in the flesh is a deceiver and the anti-christ. Such persons should not be welcomed into one's home.

## *KEY VERSES: II JOHN 7, 9, 10*

For many deceivers are entered into the world, who confess not that Jesus Christ is come in the flesh. This is a deceiver and an antichrist. Whosoever transgresseth, and abideth not in the doctrine of Christ, hath not God. He that abideth in the doctrine of Christ, he hath both the Father and the Son. If there come any unto you, and bring not this doctrine, receive him not into your house, neither bid him God speed.

## *KEY WORDS*

Truth—5 times
Love—4 times

## *OUTLINE*

| | |
|---|---|
| Verses 1-3 | Greeting |
| Verses 4-6 | Walk in truth: practical aspect—the path of the believer |
| Verses 7-11 | Watch against error: doctrinal aspect—the peril of the believer |
| Verses 12-13 | Parting |

# III JOHN

1 Chapter                                    Key Verse:
(14 Verses)                                  III John 8

### WRITTEN BY
The Apostle John from Ephesus.

### WRITTEN TO
A church elder named Gaius.

### DATE WRITTEN
Approximately 90 A.D.

### PURPOSES OF BOOK
To commend Gaius to serve in love and in truth; to
warn him about Diotrephes and his pride; and to
commend the Christian, Demetrius.

### THEME
Truth and love versus pride and strife.

### BRIEF DESCRIPTION
John commends and encourages Gaius to continue to
serve and to be hospitable both to believers and strangers. He warns him about Diotrephes. He commends
Demetrius. John presents sketches of Gaius and De-

metrius, who set good examples to follow, and of
Diotrephes, who set a bad example.

## KEY VERSE: III JOHN 8

We therefore ought to receive such, that we might be
fellow helpers to the truth.

## KEY WORD

Truth (true)—7 times

## OUTLINE

# JUDE

1 Chapter                                 Key Verses:
(25 Verses)                               Jude 3, 4

### WRITTEN BY

Jude, "servant of Jesus Christ and brother of James."
He probably was the half brother referred to in Matt.
13:55, Mark 6:3, and Gal. 1:19. He was not an Apostle (Jude 17, 18).

### WRITTEN TO

Believers in general, "sanctified ... preserved ...
called." It is possible that since Jude refers to James as
his brother, he could be writing to the same ones to
whom James wrote "the twelve tribes which are scattered abroad" (James 1:1).

### DATE WRITTEN

This letter was written after Peter wrote his second
letter (June 17, 18). If II Peter was written in 64 A.D.,
then possibly Jude wrote his in 67-68 A.D.

### PURPOSES OF BOOK

Jude wrote to instruct his readers in the common salvation; to warn of false teachers who had "crept in unawares"; to warn about the lawless; and to comfort and to encourage believers in the faith.

## THEME
"Ye should earnestly contend for the faith."

## BRIEF DESCRIPTION
There were false teachers who were introducing doctrinal error; who were lascivious and licentious; who were practicing lawlessness; and who had perverted views of divine grace and Christian liberty. Jude warns his readers about these "certain men." In his warning, Jude refers to seven Old Testament examples of wickedness and the resulting judgment (verses 5, 6, 7, 9, 11). Christians are warned to be on their guard against false teachers and, at the same time, believers are comforted and encouraged in their faith (verses 20-25).

## SPECIAL INFORMATION
Compare II Peter 2:3-3:4 with Jude. The message of Jude concerning false teachers is very similar in words, ideas and Old Testament illustrations. Judging from the statements of Jude 17, 18 and II Pet. 3:3 it seems that Jude was written after II Peter. Peter says the false teachers will come (II Pet. 3:3); Jude says they have come (Jude 4). Jude's description of the false teachers is more dismal than Peter's description in his second epistle.

## KEY VERSES: JUDE 3, 4
Beloved, when I gave all diligence to write unto you of the common salvation, it was needful for me to write unto you, and exhort you that ye should earnestly contend for the faith which was once delivered unto the saints. For there are certain men crept in

unawares, who were before of old ordained to this condemnation, ungodly men, turning the grace of our God into lasciviousness, and denying the only Lord God, and our Lord Jesus Christ.

## KEY WORD

Ungodly—5 times

## OUTLINE

| | |
|---|---|
| Verses 1, 2 | Salutation |
| Verses 3, 4 | Reason for Writing |
| Verses 5, 11 | Examples from the past showing God's hatred of sin and judgment on unbelief |
| Verses 12-19 | The false teachers characterized and their doom pictured. |
| Verses 20-25 | Exhortation and consolation for the believer |

# REVELATION

| | |
|---|---|
| 22 Chapters | Key Verses: |
| (404 Verses) | Revelation 1:18, 19 |

## WRITTEN BY

The Apostle John (Rev. 1:1, 4, 9; 22:8), from Patmos (Rev. 1:9), an island off the coast of Asia Minor.

## WRITTEN TO

The seven churches of Asia (Rev. 1:4, 11; 22:16); the servants of Jesus Christ (Rev. 1:1; 22:6); and any person, saved or unsaved, who will read and heed it (Rev. 1:3; 3:20; 22:7, 17-19).

## DATE WRITTEN

Probably between 95-98 A.D.

## PURPOSES OF BOOK

1. In the Greek the word "apocalypse" means to reveal or unveil. Rev. 1:1 states that this is "the revelation of Jesus Christ." Thus, the book was written to reveal the final and ultimate truth of the person, the power and the purpose of Jesus Christ.
2. To instruct, encourage and rebuke the professing churches. It has application for the professing church today (Rev. 2-3; 22:16).

## THEME

The Revelation of Jesus Christ (Rev. 1:1) depicting what was, what is, and what will be (Rev. 1:19).

## BRIEF DESCRIPTION

The Apostle John was banished to the Isle of Patmos for his testimony (Rev. 1:9). On the Lord's day (Sunday, not Saturday; Rev. 1:10) he was given this revelation of Jesus Christ by an angel of God from Jesus Christ, who in turn received it from God the Father (Rev. 1:1). The book is an expansion of the theme "the things which thou hast seen," (Rev. 1:9-20, "the things which are," (Rev. 2-3) "and the things which shall be hereafter" (Rev. 4-22:5).

Of the 404 verses in the book of Revelation, 278 of them refer to the Old Testament.

## SPECIAL INFORMATION
### Four Schools of Interpretation
### As to the Meaning of Revelation

1. The Praeterist view is that the greater part of the book already has been fulfilled in the early history of events of the church when John wrote, events such as the fall of Jerusalem and the reign of Nero. The seven kings of Rev. 17:10 are interpreted as being the Roman Emperors Augustus, Tiberias, Gaius (Caligula), Claudius, Nero, Galba, and Otho.
2. The Historist (Presentist) view is that the book is a detailed prophesy of church history from John's time to the end of the world.
3. The Futurist view (subscribed to by premillennialists, with some variations) is that the events in Chapter 4 through Chapter 18 have yet to occur, and that they will be fulfilled after the rapture and during the seven years' "tribulation" upon the earth, immediately prior

to the second coming of the Lord Jesus Christ to reign upon the earth for 1,000 years (the "millennium"). In Chapter 19 through Chapter 22, a view of events after the millennium and into eternity is given. Events in heaven and on earth are depicted.

4. The Spiritual (Idealist) view is that great spiritual realities are given under various symbols and that actual events are not depicted. Amillennialists (ie., no millennium) generally hold this view.

### KEY VERSES: REVELATION 1:18, 19

I am he that liveth, and was dead; and, behold, I am alive for evermore, Amen; and have the keys of hell and of death. Write the things which thou hast seen, and the things which are, and the things which shall be hereafter.

### KEY WORDS

I saw (I beheld, I looked)—49 times

### KEY WORD FOR EACH CHAPTER

1. Alpha, Omega
2. Angel
3. Angel
4. Throne
5. Lamb
6. Six seals
7. 144,000
8. Seventh seal, Four angels, Trumpets
9. Fifth, sixth angels
10. Seventh angel, Little book
11. Two witnesses
12. Woman, Dragon
13. Two beasts
14. 144,000
15. Seven angels, Plagues

16. Seven vials
17. Babylon
18. Fallen
19. Marriage
20. Great White Throne
21. New Jerusalem
22. Come

## OUTLINE

## ALTERNATE OUTLINE

## CHAPTER BY CHAPTER

Ch. 1 Prologue, and description of the Lord Jesus Christ.

Ch.  2  Letters to the churches of Ephesus, Smyrna, Pergamos, and Thyatira.

Ch.  3  Letters to the churches of Sardis, Philadelphia and Laodicea.

Ch.  4  The scene in heaven with the Lord on the throne as the Creator.

Ch.  5  The same scene but with the Lord seen as the Lion-Lamb holding the sealed book in His hand.

Ch.  6  The six seals opened.

Ch.  7  The 144,000 seen on earth; the multitude without number seen in heaven.

Ch.  8  The seventh seal opened; four of the seven angels sound their trumpets.

Ch.  9  The fifth and sixth angels sound their trumpets.

Ch. 10  The seventh angel and the little book.

Ch. 11  The two witnesses; the seventh angel sounds his trumpet.

Ch. 12  The woman and the dragon.

Ch. 13  The two beasts.

Ch. 14  The Lamb and the 144,000; the six angels.

Ch. 15  Seven angels with the seven last plagues.

Ch. 16  The seven angels pour out the seven vials.

Ch. 17  Babylon, her nature and character; the seven kings.

Ch. 18  Babylon, her fall and overthrow.

Ch. 19  Preparation for the marriage supper of the Lamb; beginning of the millennium.

Ch. 20  During the millennium; judgment of the unsaved.

Ch. 21  The new heaven and the new earth; the new Jerusalem.

Ch. 22  Description of the new Jerusalem; words of comfort and caution; epilogue.

*NOTES*

*Notes*

*Notes*

*NOTES*

*NOTES*

*NOTES*